The Watchmaker's Revenge

The incredible true story of murder, suicide and insanity in Victorian Coventry

ADAM WOOD

MANGO

All images from author's collection unless otherwise stated.

Published by

Mango Books
18 Soho Square
London
W1D 3QL

www.WatchmakerBook.com

ISBN: 978-1-914277-30-6

The Watchmaker's Revenge

For Pat and Derek Style,
who opened Pandora's box.

ACKNOWLEDGEMENTS

I've long held an interest in true crime, especially of the Victorian era. Not so much the facts of the offence itself, but how it impacts the community in which it was committed. This started when I was around twelve years old, when my grandfather, born in London's East End, told me that his father had seen the body of one of Jack the Ripper's victims. The Whitechapel murders are known around the world, but what's often overlooked is the fact that people were going about their everyday business while these horrific attacks were being committed.

But the infamous serial killer of 1888 was a rare exception. Even the briefest scan through the reports of court proceedings in any town or city across the country shows that the vast majority of defendants were ordinary people, often caught up in spur-of-the-moment decisions which backfired, such as petty theft, or assault while under the influence. Some brought before the magistrates had been driven to the edge by others, and such was the case of Oliver Style.

I've owned a copy of *The Chronicle of Crime* by my friend, the author Martin Fido, since it was published in 1995. It's a compilation of notorious crimes dating from 1820, presented year-by-year in a tabloid-style. I was recently flicking through it idly and my eye caught the word 'Coventry' in a brief entry for 1880 – I suppose it was the fact that I currently live in the city that caused it to leap off the page. I read Martin's basic 200-word account of the shootings by Oliver Style, and was surprised that I'd never seen any mention of it before.

I immediately trawled the British Newspaper Archive for contemporary reports, and was amazed to read that people connected to the case lived in streets I now walk, and drank in the same local pubs where I myself enjoy a pint. Not one, but two tragic incidents described in the following pages were played out on Hearsall Common, where I often walk my dog. I immediately felt a connection to the story, and spent some time learning about the Coventry watchmaking industry of the mid Victorian period, which is the backdrop against which the watchmaker's revenge was played out. I purchased a pocket watch made in Coventry in 1880, the year in question, to better understand the work which went into such an item by the skilled workmen who handled various elements in its production. There's a chance – albeit it extremely remote – that my watch was worked on by Oliver Style, who was a watch finisher. For their advice and insight into this honourable trade I extend my thanks to the volunteers of the Coventry Watch Museum, which is a fascinating place to visit; see www.coventrywatchmuseum.co.uk for details, and to make a donation to help them continue their important work.

With the facts of Oliver Style's horrific actions fully researched, it was time to look into his genealogy. As it always the case thanks to the *Ancestry* website, this had already been done. Oliver's great-grandson Derek, but more especially his wife Pat, had assembled a vastly detailed family tree, and I was fortunate to stumble across this during my own research. Pat had discovered the story of Oliver Style's rampage and, setting out to learn more about him from senior family members who had some first-hand knowledge, persuaded Derek to pick the brains of his mother Doris, who had married Oliver's grandson Norman Style, and his aunt Rita, Norman's brother. Luckily, they had the foresight to tape record the conversation with Rita and a transcript appears as an appendix in this book, providing much anecdotal information which simply couldn't be found in an online archive.

I'm saddened that Derek and Pat are not with us today to see their research added to and placed in its proper context of the watchmaking community of late Victorian Coventry, but extremely grateful to their daughter Alison Kukla – Oliver Style's great-great-granddaughter for kindly allowing me free access to their work, not all of it online. This includes the Style family Bible, which was hidden away for many years – possibly as a result of the shame brought by Oliver's actions – until being rediscovered in recent years. As is always the case, holding such a tangible link to the past is a thrill.

Richard Style, of another strand of the family, has also been very helpful. My thanks to both Alison and Richard for being so generous with their time and assistance.

My appreciation also to the following bodies for their kind help: Coventry Archives; Keith Bushnell and the staff of the ECHO community newspaper; the Herbert Art Gallery and Museum; and the staff at Warwick Archives. I've also appreciated the advice offered by the admin and members of the 'Bygone Spon End, Chapelfields and Nauls Mill' and 'Visit Historic Coventry' Facebook pages.

The following kind people offered help and encouragement, for which I'm grateful: Karen Ashley-Lockett; Malvern Carvell; David Green; Nikki Hagan; John Haynes; Leonard Heanes; Charlie Johnson; Tom Nixon; Mark Ripper; Ed Tooker and Lorraine Tooker.

Finally, my thanks to my wife Sue, who put up with me dragging her around Chapelfields and Spon End and excitedly telling her that someone or other had lived in a particular house in the 1800s when I should have been emptying the dishwasher.

Adam Wood
Earlsdon, Coventry
October 2021

*

Adam Wood is the author of *Swanson: The Life and Times of a Victorian Detective*, a detailed biography of the detective who was in charge of the investigation into the Jack the Ripper murders from Scotland Yard, and *Trial of Percy Lefroy Mapleton*, an examination of the notorious 1881 railway murder of Frederick Gold on the London to Brighton express. He is also co-author with Police historian Neil Bell of *Sir Howard Vincent's Police Code, 1889*, and a series of historic walking guidebooks with Blue Badge tour guide Richard Jones.

Adam is Executive Editor of *Ripperologist* magazine, the leading publication dedicated to the serious study of the Whitechapel murders and their place in social history. From 2017 to 2021 he was Editor of the *Journal* of the Police History Society.

www.AdamWoodAuthor.com

THE WATCHMAKER'S REVENGE

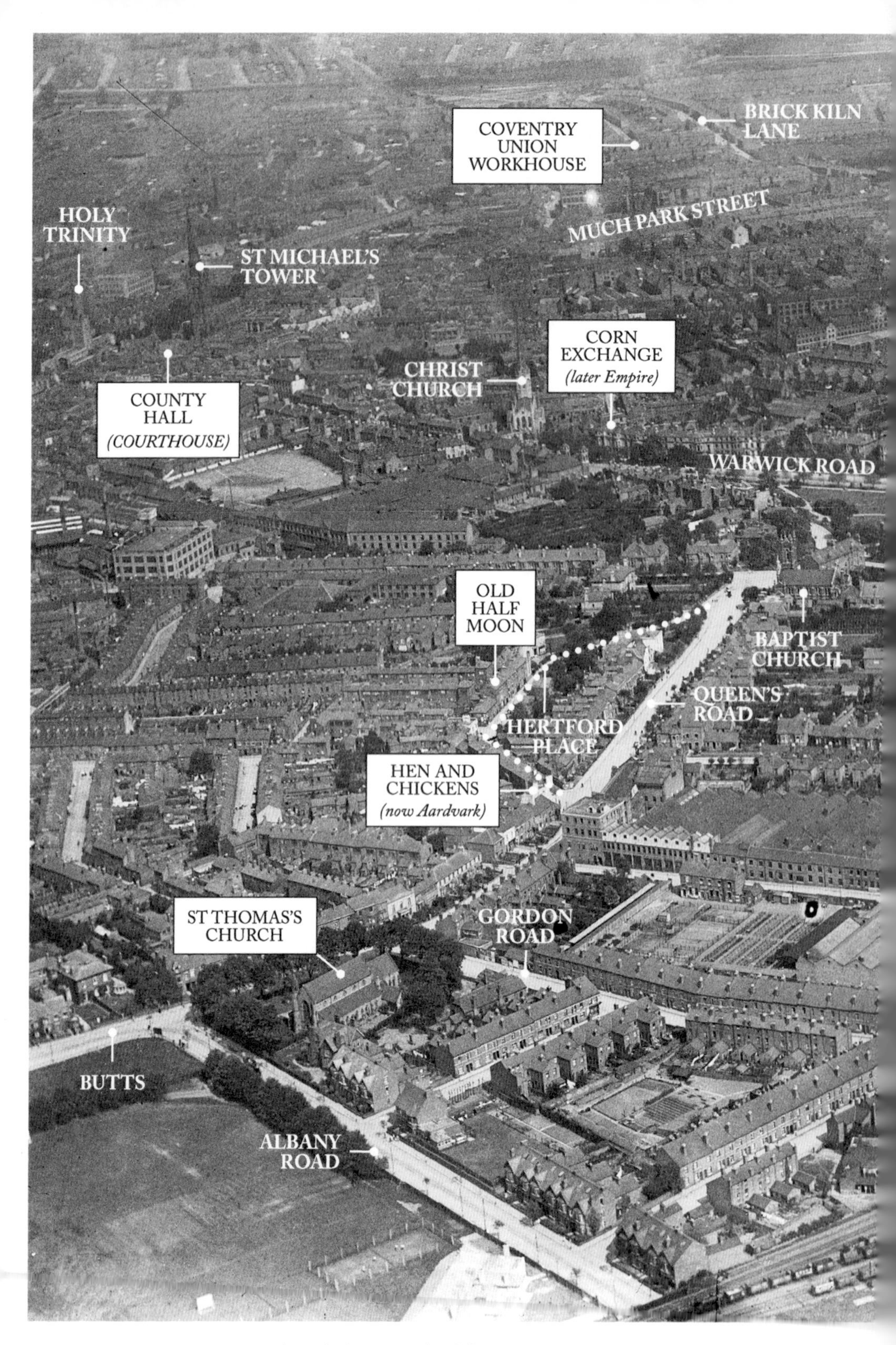

Aerial photograph of Coventry circa 1920
showing key locations in the story of the watchmaker's revenge.

INTRODUCTION

MURDEROUS OUTRAGE IN COVENTRY

> "Mrs Elkington stated that Style forced open the door, spoke to his wife, and then, turning round, called her some foul names, and said he would do for her first. He then fired a shot which wounded her in the thick of the arm above the elbow, and saying, 'You are not done for yet,' fired a second shot. The bullet struck her in the bowels, and she fell. As she was lying on the ground he fired at his wife, took hold of her by the hair of the head, and dragged her out of the house.
>
> Mrs Elkington heard another report, screamed 'Murder!' several times, and called her son. She crept along the floor and out of the house into the yard, where she became unconscious, and knew no more."

'The Murderous Outrages in Coventry',
Atherstone, Nuneaton and Warwickshire Times, 17th July 1880.

*

Reports such as the above might have been expected in London and some of the country's larger cities in the Victorian era, but such incidents were almost unheard of in industrious Coventry, whose citizens were in the main busy working in the watchmaking trade, which still employed almost 3,000 people in 1880 – the year the attack took place – despite the industry about to start its decline in the face of competition from automated watchmaking by companies in Switzerland and America.

It was an honourable trade whose workers were highly skilled, in the main decent people working hard for their families, many members of which might be employed. It was not unusual for young children – especially girls – to assist their fathers in his work, their smaller, nimbler fingers and keener eyesight better suited to the more fiddly aspects of assembly.

But not all those working in the watchmaking trade were as dependable. Skilled and hardworking they might have been but, as with any industry which has its foundations in a tightly-knit community, scratch the surface and stories of drunkenness, assault and domestic violence regularly reveal themselves. But let me be clear; the tale of the watchmaker's revenge is not an attack on that industry – that is simply the background to which it was played out.

Despite being now long-forgotten – so much so that Google doesn't produce a single result – the story of Oliver Style is an extraordinary tale of insanity, multiple attempted murder and suicide. It was widely reported in the national press, and for six months was rarely out of the pages of Coventry's newspapers. Fifty-two years later, on 23rd May 1932, in its 'Historians' Corner' column the *Midland Daily Telegraph* recalled:

> "There was a great deal of excitement in Coventry... in consequence of a murderous outrage which had been committed by a well-known watchmaker."

But this was not a case of a cold-blooded killer on the rampage in Victorian Coventry. It was an all-too-familiar story of an ordinary man with an explosive temper who felt himself pushed to the edge. At the height of his rage, having just shot his wife twice while their infant son was in her arms, Style told a witness "I have done what I intended to do; I have shot the ——— cat to the heart." Yet later, repentant at the trial, through tears he said he knew he had committed "a cruel and rascally act," and was sorry.

Yet despite the intense coverage, readers of the day were not aware of the full incredible story beyond the facts of the shootings. The lives of Oliver Style and his family were much like those of others in the 1870s and '80s, when overcrowding, drunkenness and infant mortality was common, but few had a closet which contained skeletons such as illegitimate children, suicide, manslaughter through bare-knuckle fighting and, eventually, insanity. All this and more are revealed over the following pages.

The story of Oliver Style's revenge begins not in Coventry's watchmaking district, but in the heart of London's East End.

1.

LONDON BEGINNINGS

The man who would introduce Oliver Style to the watchmaking art was his father, John George Style,[1] who was born in the capital on 15th April 1810.[2] His own father, another John,[3] was a watch finisher in Bethnal Green, East London,[4] and the skill passed to his son, as John Jr.[5]

The clock and watchmaking industry had long been established in the capital, with timepieces being produced from the sixteenth century. In 1655 an English scientist named Robert Hooke, studying the movement of pendulums in an attempt to improve their accuracy, noted the effect that gravity had on the parts and as a result managed to demonstrate a pocket watch fitted with a coil spring.

Joseph Windmill, considered one of the finest clockmakers in late

1 All records relating to John list him as 'Style' rather than 'Styles', which is how his son Oliver and other family members are often recorded due to the inconsistency of census enumerators and newspaper reporters. For consistency, I have retained use of the 'Style' spelling throughout this book, as given on all family documents.

2 John George Style was baptised at St Giles Cripplegate in the City of London on 29th July 1810. [Baptismal Register].

3 1783-1864.

4 1841 and 1851 census.

5 He is recorded as a watchmaker in 1841 census, the first available record giving his occupation, but must surely have been engaged in the industry for many years prior to this. For instance, his appearance in court in 1828 appears to allude to his stealing instruments used by his father for his own watch making.

seventeenth century London, formed a family business with his son Thomas and both were important figures in the founding of the Clockmakers' Company, which was created by Royal Charter in 1631, becoming the ruling body in watchmaking in the City of London. A watchmaker wanting to practise in the square mile had to first become a freeman of the Company. In this way the standard of quality was maintained.

Over the next two hundred years a vast number of inventions and improvements were seen from London's watchmakers, as the pocket watch became as important as an item of decorative jewellery than just a simple timepiece. This saw a new line of work open up – engraving and watch jewel makers.

While the leading watchmakers settled in the City of London, Soho in the West End had an important settlement of French watchmakers, and Clerkenwell in north London was a centre for the working classes of the trade. As would be seen half a decade later in Coventry, many streets in the district were almost fully occupied by workers engaged in the various aspects of the watchmaking trade.[6]

The Style family, practising in the art of watchmaking in the early nineteenth century, were no doubt like many of the period; picking up work in the Clerkenwell district but unable to afford to live there, so took accommodation a little to the east in places like Bethnal Green, Hoxton and Shoreditch.

There appears to have been no love lost between father and son; the Newgate Calendar of Prisoners for 1828 lists 'John Style the younger' – aged eighteen at the time – being brought to court by his father for 'stealing a pair of pliers and other articles' belonging to the older man. Thankfully, John George was allowed to walk free when no strong evidence was presented.[7] What this meant to the relationship between father and son can be imagined. When John Sr died aged eighty-one, on 11th January 1864, it was at the Clock

6 *WatchPro* magazine, January 2013.
7 Newgate Calendar of Prisoners, 1785-1853. Piece 35: 1828.

Clock and Watchmakers' Asylum, where John Style Sr died in 1864.
Courtesy Wellcome Institute

and Watchmakers' Asylum[8] in East Barnet, north London[9], with his son by then long removed to Coventry.

A year after his court appearance John George Style married Maria Pearson at All Saints, Maidstone, on 20th October 1829.[10] The groom was nineteen years old, the bride – from Shadwell, east London – twenty-three.[11] Whether she was aware of his brush with the law at the hands of his father earlier is unknown. The witnesses were William Pearson, the bride's brother – six years her junior – and Ann Woodhams.[12]

8 Death certificate of John Style, registered 14th January 1864.

9 The Asylum, which opened in 1858, was a refuge for elderly watch and clockmakers and their widows. It was close to Colney Hatch Lunatic Asylum, which had opened seven years earlier. The Clock and Watchmakers' Asylum was demolished in the late 1950s.

10 England, Select Marriages, 1538–1973. FHL Film Number: 1835448. Reference ID: p11, 33.

11 Maria Pearson born 15th September 1806 and was baptised at St Dunstan and All Saints, Stepney, on 5th October. [Baptismal Register].

12 England, Select Marriages, 1538–1973. FHL Film Number: 1835448. Reference ID: p11, 33.

The riddle as to why the young couple would travel to Kent to tie the knot was solved when a son, John William Style, was baptised there five days after the nuptials.[13]

The family returned to London, and Hoxton in the East End, but tragedy was to strike early in 1833 when young John William died. He was buried in the churchyard of St John the Baptist, Hoxton on 27th February 1833.[14]

After shedding their tears, the couple wasted no time in starting a new family. Their daughter Mary Ann was born in 1834,[15] followed by a son, William, on 6th February 1837.[16]

Once again, tragedy struck. Maria and her children, just two years old and eight months respectively, were admitted to Camden Workhouse on 12th October 1837.[17] Perhaps they were ill, and seeking attention at the workhouse infirmary; William certainly seems to have been ailing, for he was hastily baptised on 5th December[18] but died the following day. He was just ten months old. Maria and Mary Ann were discharged to be reunited with John on 15th December.[19]

Another son, named William Henry in remembrance, was born in 1839,[20] and early in 1841 the family welcomed Matilda.[21] In the census taken that year they were recorded as living at Sun Street, close to where Liverpool Street railway station would be opened thirty-four years later.

Throughout the preceding years John and Maria had moved

13 Baptismal Register of All Saints, Maidstone, 25th October 1829.
14 Church of England Deaths and Burials, 1813-2003. Although burials were recorded, death certificates were not mandatory until July 1837, so we are unable to discover the exact date and cause of little John's premature demise.
15 Year of birth established from Mary Ann's stated age in the 1841 census.
16 Baptismal record for William Style.
17 Camden Workhouse Register, 1818-1843.
18 Baptismal record for William Style.
19 Camden Workhouse Register, 1818-1843.
20 Age taken from 1841, 1851 and 1861 census returns.
21 The 1841 census, taken on 6th June, records Matilda as being five months old, ie born in January.

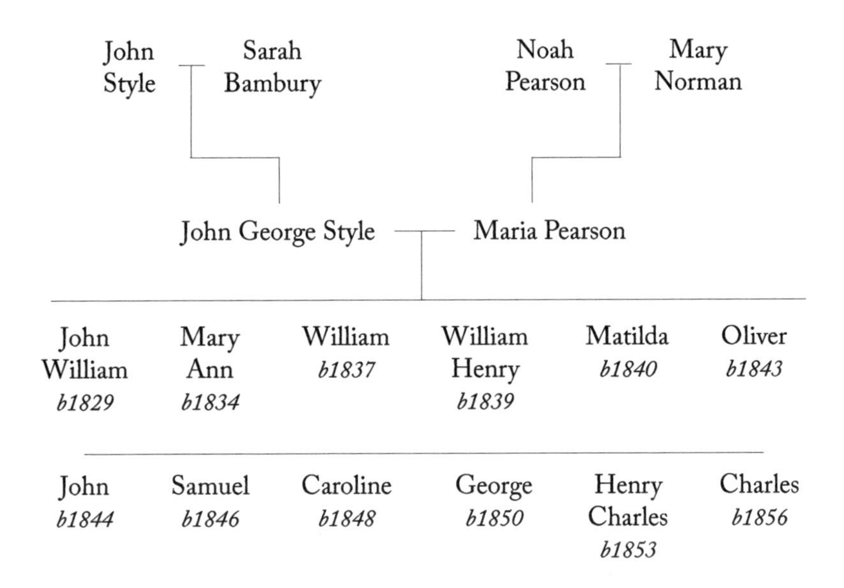

their young family between north and east London, no doubt following work in the watchmaking trade where it could be found as the industry began to decline in the capital. By the early 1840s they were living at 29 New York Street, Bethnal Green, and it was here that another son, Oliver, was born on 19th January 1843. It's tempting to take the location of his birth as an omen for future events, as the entrance to New York Street was opposite Bethnal Green Police Station. Oliver was registered by his mother on 1st March.[22]

When Oliver was barely a year old,[23] John decided to move the family out of London, which had seen a dramatic slump in its watchmaking fortunes since its heyday of the early 1800s as timepieces made in Switzerland had become more popular than

22 Birth certificate of Oliver Style.

23 Brother John was born at Coventry in December 1844, indicating that he had been conceived between around March of that year, with Oliver having recently celebrated his first birthday.

Bethnal Green.

those made in the capital. In 1842, the year before Oliver's birth, 99,000 gold and silver watches were hallmarked in London – less than half that produced fifty years earlier, when 191,678 were hallmarked in 1796.[24]

John turned his gaze toward another busy centre of watchmaking, to Coventry, where the industry was still booming.

The family no doubt travelled to the city in the hope that John would secure more regular work, but it was a decision which would in time impact the lives of many, and not just the Style family.

24 'England: Where watchmaking all began' by Rob Corder, *WatchPro* magazine, 15th January 2013.

2.

BLOOD ON SPON END

Despite boasting a much smaller population than London, Coventry was an important city in a strategic location. By the fourteenth century it was the centre of the cloth trade. It was one of the largest and most important cities in England in the Middle Ages, and in fact had served as the country's capital more than once, first when Henry IV summoned a Parliament in Coventry in 1404.

While the cloth industry remained of great importance to the city, especially ribbon weaving, by the early nineteenth century Coventry had become one of the three main British centres of watch and clock manufacture alongside Prescot in Lancashire and Clerkenwell, thanks to its central location which made it perfect for the transportation of watches and parts across the country.

The city's main areas for the watchmaking community grew around Spon Street, to the south, where important figures Samuel Vale and then Richard Rotherham ran hugely successful businesses, and the Gosford Street area in the inner city.

But in the main those working in the industry were self-employed, offering a huge variety of different skills in all parts of the chain. It's estimated that there were more than seventy different roles in the manufacture of a single watch, with one man producing the movement itself, another the case, a third the enamelled face, while yet a fourth hand-painted the numerals, and so on. The watch finisher would be responsible for putting all the parts together, and setting the balance so that the movement ran correctly. Each of these tasks was a highly skilled job.

The Coventry Watchmakers' Association was formed in 1858 to protect the wages of its members, ensuring that prices were set across the board for each role – thereby eliminating the possibility of undercutting a rival for any particular job.[25]

After the errand boys, the lowest rung was the apprentice – a boy who, on leaving school aged thirteen or fourteen, would be employed by a skilled master to learn the trade. This was often the boy's father, which kept the wages paid to a minimum.

An apprentice was often kept at the most basic task of polishing the components for more than a year, familiarising himself with each part, before being allowed to move on to more advanced work. For a young man this was mind-numbing in its boredom, and a number of apprentices found themselves in trouble with their masters for failure to turn up for work, as we shall see.

After serving the full apprenticeship – a seven year term – the now fully-qualified craftsman would often work for a year or two at another watchmaker's premises to round out his experience, before taking on the top jobs himself. This would make him around twenty-three years old, and it was at this time that many young men felt their prospects were at the highest potential and he was therefore in a position to marry and start a family.[26]

*

It was into this thriving industry that the Style family settled, first in Hill Street to the west of the city centre. A son, John, was born there in December 1844; the first of the family born in Coventry.[27] Samuel joined them in 1846.[28]

By 1848 the family were well established in Coventry, with John picking up work regularly in the Spon Street area of the city.

25 See *Moments in Time: The History of the Coventry Watch Industry Volume 1* by the Coventry Watch Museum Project Limited (5th Edition: 2014) for a detailed examination of the Coventry watchmaking industry.

26 See *Brown Boots in Earlsdon* by Mary Montes (Coventry and Warwickshire Historical Association Pamphlet No. 15).

27 John Style Jr was born at Hill Street, Coventry on 23rd December 1844. Birth certificate, registered by his father on 31st December 1844.

28 Birth Index, 1837-1915: Samuel Style, Q3 1846.

WATCHMAKERS' ASSOCIATION.

THE Committee of the Watchmakers' Association, in the List now submitted to the general body of the Watch Trade, (as passed at a Public Meeting of the Association, held in Saint Mary's Hall, April 5, 1859,) have endeavoured so to frame it as to meet the present great necessity so generally admitted by Manufacturers and Workmen of an uniform rate of payment, for the same class and quality of work, and solicit for it that due consideration its importance so urgently demands, feeling confident that its adoption will be alike advantageous to the Employer and Employed, by affording that security, which, based upon mutual confidence, must prove beneficial to all engaged in the Trade, and demonstrate to each the great value of an established List.

In forming this List the Committee have not, in any case, adopted the highest rate which is being paid in Coventry, but have fixed a *minimum* price, below which they think the work cannot be done honestly and well. It is to the man of average ability (those of superior abilities can generally command a good price for their work.) and the honourable Manufacturer that the establishment of a List would be of most importance; inasmuch as it would shield them from that crushing competition which, in times of temporary depression has a tendency to injure both; therefore, to the Manufacturer who wishes well to the workman as well as his trade they think such a List will be acceptable, and they, (the Committee) hope shortly to be able to announce a Conference of Manufacturers and Workmen to consider the desirability of its immediate adoption.

By order of the Committee,

Committee Room, Rose Inn, Moat Street,
14th June, 1859.

CHARLES SHUFFLEBOTHAM,
Chairman.

FINISHER'S LIST OF LOWEST PRICES

VERGE WORK.

	s.	d.	
That the lowest price paid for finishing a Verge Watch, be	10	0	
If jewelled in cock and pottance ..	1	0	*Extra*
If seconds train	1	0	*Extra*

LEVER WORK, FULL PLATE.

	s.	d.	
That the lowest price paid for finishing a Grey* Lever Watch, going barrel or otherwise, be	12	0	
When given out in Three parts.			
For First part..	3	9	
For Escapement	3	9	
For Finishing off	4	6	
When given out in Two parts.			
For First part and pivoting Escapement	5	6	
For Finishing off	6	6	
If Reversed movement	1	0	*Extra*
If Screw pillars	0	6	*Extra*
If Sprung above the Balance.. ..	1	0	*Extra*
Jewelled holes, per pair	0	6	*Extra*
Jewelled on End pieces	1	0	*Extra*
10 Size Movements and under ..	2	0	*Extra*
20 Size Movements and upwards ..	1	0	*Extra*
That the lowest price paid for finishing a Glossed-frame Watch, not Glossed Fusee hollow, be	18	0	
When given out in Three parts			
For First part..	5	6	
For Escapement	5	6	
For Finishing off	7	0	
When given out in Two parts.			
For First part and pivoting Escapement	8	6	
For Finishing off	9	6	
If Reversed Movement	1	0	*Extra*
If Screw pillars	0	6	*Extra*
If Sprung above the Balance ..	2	0	*Extra*
Jewelled holes, per pair	1	0	*Extra*
Jewelled on End pieces, per pair ..	1	6	*Extra*
10 Sizes and under	2	0	*Extra*

LEVER WORK, ¾ PLATE.

	£.	s.	d.	
That the lowest price paid for finishing a Grey ¾ plate Watch, be	1	5	0	
When given out in Three parts.				
For First part	0	7	0	
For Escapement	0	7	0	
For Finishing off	0	11	0	
When given out in Two parts.				
For First part & pivoting Escapement	0	10	6	
For Finishing off	0	14	6	
Jewelled holes, per pair	0	1	0	*Extra*
Jewelled on End pieces	0	1	6	*Extra*
If Capped	0	1	0	*Extra*
If lower in height of pillars than 0/4	0	2	0	*Extra*
10 Sizes and under.. ..	0	2	0	*Extra*
That the lowest price paid for finishing a Glossed ¾ plate Watch, be	1	12	0	
If hollow pinion and fusee	1	15	0	
When given out in Two parts				
For Escapement	0	12	0	
For First half and Finishing off ..	1	3	0	
Jewelled holes, per pair ..	0	1	0	*Extra*
Jewelled with End pieces ..	0	1	6	*Extra*
If Capped	0	1	0	*Extra*
If lower in height of pillars than 0/4	0	2	0	*Extra*
10 Sizes and under ..	0	3	0	*Extra*

CENTRE SECONDS WORK.

	£.	s.	d.
That the lowest price paid for finishing a Glossed Centre Seconds Watch, be	2	5	0
When given out in Two parts.			
For Escapement	0	14	0
First part and Finishing off ..	1	11	0

* In using the term Grey Work it is to be understood to apply to the making of Pivots and Shoulders, without using pivot polishers.

Spon End.

On the night of Saturday, 15th January that year he had been out with friends, and in the early hours of the Sunday was sitting in a house on Spon End belonging to a Mrs Paget,[29] who offered bread and bacon to hungry late night visitors.

There were four or five friends sitting quietly enjoying a late supper accompanied by a drop of hot elder wine,[30] when a young man named John Stokes[31] entered and asked for some toasted bacon. John Style offered a glass of wine to the newcomer, who had clearly had enough already, but was rudely refused. On being served his bacon Stokes loudly complained about the quality, and began to

29 Possibly Susannah Paget, fifty-one years old in 1848, who lived at No. 84 Spon End with her watchmaker husband John and their children. [1851 and 1861 census returns].

30 *Coventry Herald and Observer*, 18th January 1848.

31 John Stokes was born to ribbon weaver Daniel and his wife Ann of Spon End, and baptised on 1st March 1829. He was working in the street as a watch finisher by the time of the 1851 census, three years after his attack on John Style.

annoy the other diners.[32]

John Style, sitting opposite on the other side of the table, told him to keep the noise down, otherwise he would put him outside.[33]

Just then Mrs Paget went upstairs, and Stokes got up to walk around to the other side of the table. Thinking he was going outside into the yard, John stood up to let him pass but immediately felt a sharp stab under the left ear, inflicted by Stokes using the knife he had been eating with. Blood spurted out a yard in front of the wounded man, and he began to collapse to the floor. One of his friends, William Harrow,[34] caught hold of John, saying, "My dear fellow sit down, you will be a dead man."[35]

Constable Samuel Holmes was sent for. On arrival he found John very faint, and unable to see. He was still bleeding profusely. PC Holmes asked who had been the perpetrator, to which Style replied that he would be able to tell the man by his voice. Stokes was told to state his name, and in this way he was identified by the wounded man.[36]

Local surgeon Edward Bicknell[37] arrived around three o'clock in the morning, and found John sitting in a coal cupboard with his head over a bucket, no doubt so positioned to catch the drops of blood. There was a large pool of blood on the floor where he had been stabbed.

The surgeon discovered a deep wound three-quarters of an inch long, directly under the left ear, and the carotid artery punctured. John was taken home in a perilous condition and told to get bed rest; he started vomiting, which caused blood to recommence flowing from the wound. Fearing the worst, Dr Bicknell sent him

32 *Coventry Standard*, 28th January 1848.

33 *Coventry Herald and Observer*, 18th January 1848.

34 Thirty-two year old William Harrow was a weaver, married to Elizabeth. [1851 census].

35 *Coventry Standard*, 28th January 1848.

36 *Coventry Herald and Observer*, 18th January 1848.

37 Forty-two year old Edward Bicknell had a practice at nearby 33 Union Street, now called Windsor Street. [Trade Directories].

to the Coventry and Warwickshire Hospital.[38]

Another watchmaker friend, Thomas Gee,[39] found the bloodied knife – a common pocket-knife – under a table and handed it to Constable Parker, who had joined his colleague.

The following morning another officer, PC Payne, went to Stokes's parents' house on Sherbourne Street and apprehended the youth.[40] His hands were wet, and he told the officer that he had just washed the blood from them.[41] On being told he was under arrest for the attack, Stokes asked "Is the man dead?" and began to cry. He was taken to the Police station.[42]

On the Monday – 17th January – magistrates heard from Mr Knott, the House Surgeon at the Hospital, that although John Style was stable, it was by no means certain whether he would survive.[43]

Stokes was remanded for a week, but on Monday the 24th the Bench received word via a note from Knott that while his wound was nearly healed, Style would be unable to appear until the Wednesday. When the hearing opened Constable Holmes testified how he had taken possession of John's shirt and neckerchief, and presented them to the magistrates,

> "the sight of which caused a thrill of horror to the mind of everyone in the Court. They were completely saturated with blood."[44]

With all the evidence heard, Stokes was committed for trial at the Warwickshire Assizes, where he was unsurprisingly found Guilty

38 At the time in Little Park Street [*Kelly's Directory*]. The hospital moved to new premises on Stoney Stanton Road in 1867 at a cost of more than £5,000 (£350,000 today).

39 Although named 'Thomas Jee' on all newspaper reports of the incident, he was Thomas Gee, a watch finisher aged thirty-five, married to Elizabeth. [1851 census].

40 *Coventry Standard*, 28th January 1848.

41 *Coventry Herald and Observer*, 31st March 1848.

42 *Coventry Standard*, 28th January 1848.

43 *Coventry Herald and Observer*, 18th January 1848.

44 *Coventry Standard*, 28th January 1848.

and sentenced to one month's imprisonment with hard labour.[45]

John Stokes' sentence was added to the Criminal Registers, but it was not the first time his name had appeared there. In 1843, aged just fourteen, he had appeared in court charged with burglary, but was found Not Guilty.[46]

The life-or-death nature of John Style's injury must have been a worry for Maria, even more so than usual, as she was pregnant at the time; Caroline was born a few months later, on 12th May 1848, at Sherbourne Street.[47] She was followed on 19th September 1850 by another brother, George.[48]

In early 1851 John Style made another appearance at Coventry Police Court, but this time as a defendant. Mr Samuel Wakefield told magistrates on 16th January that his son was apprenticed to Style as a watch finisher, but had not been paid what amounted to a substantial amount of money in wages due – some £1 3s. John was ordered to pay 18s 9d immediately, which represented the wages due up to that week, and also 5s costs.[49]

Surprisingly, despite this the young apprentice remained with the watchmaker. But in September Joseph Wakefield[50] was reported to the magistrates by John for not turning up for work. In response, he said that he had stayed away at his father's insistence, as he was often still not receiving his wages on time. Father Samuel told magistrates that it was not the first, second, or even third time that payment had not been forthcoming.

Magistrates Ralphs and Rotherham told John that he must pay the agreed wages weekly, as per the contract, but advised Joseph that he also had a duty to undertake the work, at the hours and

45 *Coventry Herald and Observer*, 31st March 1848.

46 Criminal Registers, 1791-1892: Warwickshire, 1843.

47 Birth certificate of Caroline Style, registered 22nd May 1848.

48 Birth certificate of George Style, registered 28th September 1850.

49 *Coventry Herald and Observer*, 17th January 1851.

50 Joseph John Wakefield was seventeen years old at the time of the 1851 census, and is recorded as a watch finisher living at Sherbourne Street with his parents and five siblings. He married Rebecca Bailey on 12th October 1860, by this time living on Spon Street. He died in 1875 aged just forty-one.

days agreed.

The case was dismissed, with costs divided.[51]

More followed.

Four months later, on 1st January 1852, Maria joined her husband in court. On 29th December[52] she had been at home on Harnall Row and seemingly harassed by her youngest children; baby George was just a few months old, Samuel four and Caroline two, with William, Matilda, Oliver and John all at school. She threatened to put one of them "behind the fire", at which another shrieked "Murder!"[53]

The neighbours, understandably alarmed at hearing such a cry in the claustrophobic tenements, went to investigate. One, thirty-five year old James Reading, who lived two doors along,[54] went into the Style home to see what the commotion was. Still in a temper, Maria ordered him out – "using the foulest language" – at which point husband John appeared and, on being told by his wife that Reading had "ill-used her in her own home," attacked the other man.[55]

Reading was no saint – he had served six months' imprisonment for breaking into a shop in October 1844[56] – and he defended himself admirably. His lodger, twenty-five year old ribbon weaver Selina Keen,[57] arrived to see what was happening and was attacked by Maria for her trouble, but managed to land a blow of her own, resulting in the black eye which Mrs Style now exhibited in court.

After hearing much contradictory evidence, magistrates Hawkes, Ralphs and Morris dismissed the case and divided the costs.[58]

51 *Coventry Herald and Observer*, 5th September 1851.
52 *Coventry Standard*, 2nd January 1852.
53 *Coventry Herald and Observer*, 2nd January 1852.
54 1851 census, which shows James Reading living on Harnall Row with his wife Sarah and their children Hannah and Thomas.
55 *Coventry Herald and Observer*, 2nd January 1852.
56 Criminal Registers: Warwickshire, 1844.
57 1851 census. Selina Keen married William Beckett on 3rd September 1859, the couple having two children, George and Mary Ann ('Polly').
58 *Coventry Standard*, 2nd January 1852.

Broadgate.

Did John learn his lesson? No, he did not.

In February 1855 he appeared before the magistrates charged with knocking some cakes off the head of a servant of baker Mr Hough, presumably delicately balanced on a tray. John was fined 6s with 10s 6d costs, which covered the cost of the lost pastries.[59]

Seven months later he was arrested by Inspector Vice on Coventry's Broadgate for refusing to move on after being warned for harassing a Mr Atkins, who was preaching in the square. John's defence at the Police Court the following day, 7th September, was reported in the *Coventry Standard*:

> "Style said [that] when he came up Mr Atkins was saying a great deal about Hell and Damnation, and he merely said to him, 'Parson, what might the text be?' But he should not have interfered with him at all if he had not had a glass or two."

He was ordered to contribute a shilling to the poor box.[60]

59 *Coventry Standard*, 16th February 1855.
60 *Coventry Standard*, 7th September 1855.

The following week he once again appeared, charged by Mrs Mary Eaves with threatening to "knock her head off." Once again, the *Coventry Standard* got to the heart of the matter:

> "Mr Holt, for the defendant, said they were neighbours, and had been on the best of terms before, but [Style] was drunk at the time, and did not know whether he threatened her or not."

After promising not to interfere with Mrs Eaves again, John was fined 9s costs.[61]

Perhaps this very public display of drunkenness was the result of the family having lost another child at a young age. His son Henry Charles Style had been born in 1853, but sadly died on 25th March 1855, after suffering for six days through *scarlatina maligna*, a severe strain of scarlet fever.[62] It would not have been a surprise if John had begun drinking more heavily as a result.

The following year, on 17th September 1856, hearts were healed when the final addition to the family arrived, with Charles Henry Style being born at Spon End.[63]

*

Oliver Style, thirteen years old by the time Charles was born, was probably already employed in some capacity, perhaps assisting his father with his watch finishing work as an apprentice.

He certainly had followed in his father's footsteps in more ways that one, for in 1859 he made own his first appearance in the city's newspapers – and its prison cells – following an unsavoury incident which revealed his ready temper. The apple evidently didn't fall far from the tree.

Covering the events at the city Police Court of Wednesday, 23rd November, the *Coventry Herald* reported:

61 *Coventry Standard*, 14th September 1855.
62 Death certificate of Henry Charles Style, registered 27th March 1855.
63 Birth certificate of Charles Style, registered 11th October 1856.

> "Oliver Style, a diminutive youth of 17,[64] was charged with assaulting Susannah Sankey, a young woman, on the 17th of November. The complainant called to the defendant on the day in question to ask him to explain some very uncomplimentary observations he had made concerning her.
>
> The only explanation the defendant condescended to give came in the shape of two or three violent blows in the face, and he now declined to make any effort to compromise the case. He was fined 5s and costs, and was sent to prison for 14 days in default."[65]

Another reporter wrote that Miss Sankey, who was twenty-one,[66] had called Oliver into a brewhouse – the name of which or location sadly not recorded – and "high words ensued" before he struck her.[67]

It's clear that, even at this early age, Oliver Style had a very short fuse, and would escalate into violence at the slightest provocation. The 'battle scars' earned during his youth were recorded years later on his discharge from prison,[68] which described him as having scratches on the left side of his face and forehead, the bridge of his nose, and the palm of his left hand. He had at some stage lost part of the forefinger on his left hand, but it can be clearly seen in his 'new prisoner' photograph taken on his arrival at Pentonville Prison in 1880 that he was already missing the final third of his finger. Was this caused by a work accident, or something more sinister?

Thankfully, Susannah Sankey appears not to have been affected by the attack, and went on to enjoy a long and happy life. Just eighteen months after her appearance in court she married watch finisher

64 Oliver was actually sixteen at the time of the incident. We have no record as to how 'diminutive' he was. His height would normally have been recorded in the Criminal Registers, but was not – for reasons which will be revealed.

65 *Coventry Herald*, 26th November 1859.

66 Susannah Sankey was baptised on 15th April 1838 at Chilvers Coton. She is recorded as being thirteen years old in the census of 1851, when she was living with her family at Stoneleigh.

67 *Coventry Standard*, 25th November 1859.

68 Registers of Habitual Criminals and Police Gazettes, 1834-1934: Habitual Criminals Register, 1900.

West Orchard Street.

Joseph Barnett at Coventry Registry Office,[69] on 27th April 1861, the couple eventually having six children.[70]

As for Oliver, three weeks before his victim's nuptials he was staying at the home of a sixty-five year old widow named Ellen Jones on Bromsgrove Street, Birmingham. The reason he had temporarily left Coventry is not clear; the census taken on 7th April 1861 records him as a nineteen year old watchmaker, one of three lodgers along with husband and wife William and Anne Beauchamp.[71]

Missing from the 1861 census was Oliver's father John George Style; mother Maria is recorded as a widow living at West Orchard Street with the younger children, keeping a roof above their heads by taking in laundry.

The children were taking their early steps in their respective careers. Son William, now twenty-two, was working as a watch

69 *Coventry Times*, 1st May 1861.

70 Henry (b1868), Lucy (b1871), Mary Ann (b1874), Joseph (b1876), Emma (b1878) and Charlotte (b1880). Husband Joseph Barnett died in 1889; there appears to be no record of Susannah's own passing.

71 1861 census.

finisher; Matilda, twenty, a silk weaver; John, sixteen, a watch case springer. The youngest – Samuel (fourteen), George (ten) and Charles (four) – were receiving an education.[72]

Daughter Caroline, now thirteen years old, was apprenticed to Martha McDermot, a silk weaver on Holyhead Road, and she is listed on the 1861 census as a lodger there with Martha and her husband John, a Police constable.[73]

The couple, in their fifties, had taken an interest in Caroline's welfare some two or three years earlier, after her father had reportedly deserted the family.[74] Her mother Maria was no doubt glad when they offered to take her in and teach her a skill, it being one less mouth to feed.

But shortly after the census of 1861 things went wrong. One day in September Caroline found the key to the drawer in the couple's bedroom, in which they kept their money. Taking a sovereign, she immediately went to local shops and spent most of it on a pair of boots and other items of clothing.[75]

It did not take Constable McDermot long to discover what had happened, and she was brought up before the magistrates. Reporting the court appearance, newspapers described her as "clean and decently-dressed"[76] and "a decent-looking girl"[77] – the efforts of her benefactors obvious to all. It's all very reminiscent of Oliver Twist being rescued from poverty by Mr Brownlow into a comfortable, happy existence.

Similarly, the kindly McDermot asked that she be spared any

72 1861 census.

73 John McDermot had served previously with the Birmingham Police, and was transferred to the Coventry City Police after more than a dozen years' service. He worked his way up to Sergeant and then Inspector, being warmly described in the *Coventry Standard* of 11th January 1868 as an "old and efficient police officer". He and Martha continued to live on the Holyhead Road until he died in 1887 aged seventy-nine. Martha followed in 1891.

74 We have no report confirming John George Style absconding, nor a death certificate.

75 *Coventry Times*, 25th September 1861.

76 *Coventry Times*, 25th September 1861.

77 *Coventry Standard*, 20th September 1861.

punishment, but instead be placed in the Reformatory at Tile Hill,[78] where she could continue her rehabilitation in society.

But a letter to the editor of the *Coventry Herald* signed by 'A Magistrate' in response to their coverage of Caroline's court hearing clarified that the purpose of these reformatories, of which there were four in Warwickshire, was to "reclaim children who are corrupted, often either homeless or who having parents lead them into crime."[79] As Caroline was neither, a place could not be found for her. The Bench appealed to McDermot to give her another chance, and he consented. For her part, Caroline "promised to be a good girl for the future." She was severely cautioned and discharged.[80]

But evidently the cosy domestic arrangements did not last. Within five years Caroline was back living with her family, and back in court.

The *Coventry Standard* of 13th October 1866 reported that she had summoned her eldest brother William, complaining that he had punched her in the eye on the morning of 5th October. William denied the assault, adding that

> "He had been not only a brother but a father to all his sisters. There was no father, and he had been obliged, on many occasions, to quell quarrels between the sisters, who lived with their mother."

The Bench heard evidence that Caroline was "a girl of not very good character"[81] – no doubt a reference to her stealing from the kindly McDermots, and probably more incidents not recorded. But with no witnesses produced, the case against William was dropped.

The sisters contributing to the ongoing friction with Caroline were Mary Ann and Matilda, by now thirty-two and twenty-six respectively, with Matilda having previously left the family home but now back as a mother to two year old Henry, his father

78 Ibid.
79 'Letters to the Editor', *Coventry Herald*, 4th October 1861.
80 *Coventry Times*, 25th September 1861.
81 *Coventry Standard*, 13th October 1866.

unknown.[82]

Add mother Maria, and brothers Samuel (eighteen) and Charles (eight), to the mix, and it was no doubt a tense household.

The whereabouts of father John George Style are a mystery. He is named on the apprenticeship record of son John Jr dated 13th January 1857, but nothing beyond that. There is a 'John Style' who died on 10th January 1860 at Maidstone, Kent, where he and Maria had married some thirty-one years earlier, but this man was a farm labourer, and according to the death certificate ten years older than John George would have been. Present at the death was a lady named Mary Brooker, who registered the event on 14th January 1860.[83]

John George Style's son Oliver, the last of the children born in Bethnal Green, returned to Coventry shortly after the census of 1861 and soon assumed the role of head of his own family.

But before he did, he made another appearance before the magistrates at the Coventry Police Court, charged with assaulting another watchmaker named William Bradshaw.

Oliver's elder brother William Style had been working at Bradshaw's workshop,[84] when on 27th October 1862 a row broke out about money. Nineteen year old Oliver happened to walk into the room at that moment, and naturally stuck up for his brother. William Bradshaw told the Bench that the two Style brothers had assaulted him, but Oliver said it had been self defence as a result of the older man striking him with a poker.

With no firm evidence either way the case was dismissed with costs divided,[85] but it wouldn't be long before Oliver was in trouble again – this time with much more serious implications.

82 Henry Charles Style was born on 3rd September 1864 at Buck Street, Birmingham. In the baptismal register his mother is listed as Matilda, with no father's name given.

83 Death certificate of John Style.

84 The 1861 census shows William Bradshaw living at Sovereign Place, leading off the Butts to Broomfield Place. It was later renamed Sovereign Row.

85 *Coventry Standard*, 1st November 1862.

3.

TILL DEATH US DO PART

In 1851, around the time that Oliver's father John George Style appeared in court charged with non-payment of his apprentice's wages, the Coventry Freehold Land Society purchased thirty acres of farmland to the south of the Butts, which at the time represented the southernmost perimeter of the city of Coventry.

People had escaped to the area at weekends to enjoy the clean air of what was the countryside, compared to the overcrowded courts and alleys of the city centre, and the district soon became a desirable place to live as expansion rapidly took place from 1853 onwards. The new suburb became known as Earlsdon.[86]

It would eventually be incorporated into the City in 1890, but it would not be until 1898, when Albany Road was constructed,[87] that the city's tramlines could be extended into Earlsdon and thus provide easy access for shoppers and other visitors. Before then, the most direct route to Earlsdon was via a path called Elsdon Jetty, which ran south from the Butts.[88]

On the eastern corner of this junction was St Thomas's Church,

86 See *The Coventry We Have Lost: Earlsdon and Chapelfields Explored* (2011) by David Fry and Albert Smith for a description of the development of Earlsdon.

87 Albany Road was opened on 1st December 1898. It was named after the Duchess of Albany following her visit to St Thomas's Church in November.

88 See www.earlsdon.org.uk and www.coventrysociety.org.uk for a wealth of information on the history of Earlsdon, and *The Coventry We Have Lost: Earlsdon and Chapelfields Explored* (2011) by David Fry and Albert Smith.

St Thomas's, Butts, where Oliver Style married Harriett Elkington.

constructed for the watchmaking community of Spon End and the Butts[89] out of red sandstone from Lord Leigh's quarry on the Kenilworth Road to a design by the architects Sharpe and Paley, and consecrated by the Bishop of Coventry on 7th August 1849. Reporting on the occasion, one local newspaper commented:

> "The new church, which has thus been set apart for the worship of God, is an edifice of which we can justly speak in terms of high praise."[90]

It was at St Thomas's,[91] fifteen years later, that Oliver Style married

89 *The Coventry Watchmakers' Heritage Trail: A Guided Walk Through the Watchmaking Areas of Spon End and Chapelfields in Coventry* by the Coventry Watch Museum Project Limited (3rd Revised Edition: 2014)

90 *Coventry Standard*, 10th August 1849.

91 St Thomas's served the parish for one hundred and twenty-four years. Despite being granted Grade II listing, by the early 1970s it was no longer in ecclesiastical use and was demolished in 1976 to make way for a housing complex, St Thomas's Court, which today provides thirty-six retirement flats. The Warden's House is the former vicarage, built in 1897.

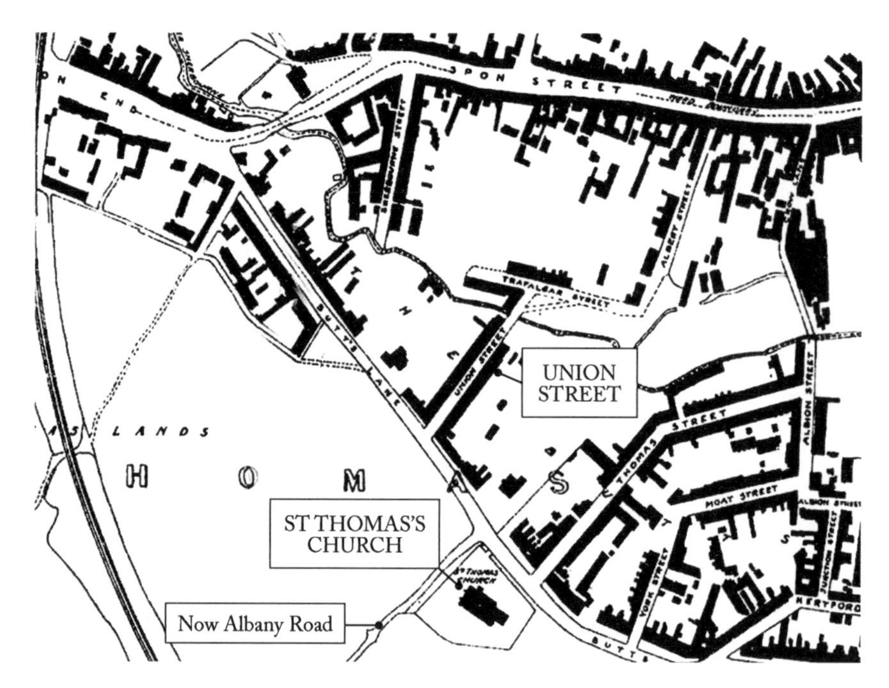

1851 map showing St Thomas's on Butts Lane and Union Street, where both bride and groom were residing at the time of their marriage.

Harriett Elkington, on Monday, 1st August 1864.[92]

He would have not long completed his apprenticeship, and then spent a further year or two gaining experience before taking on the top-paid work.[93] At the age of twenty-two Oliver Style now felt ready to provide for a wife – or, as we shall soon hear, perhaps he felt that he had to.

Harriett had been born on 5th September 1845 at Coventry's Much Park Street to father Thomas and mother Ann.[94]

Six siblings had already been born to the couple; James,[95] Emma,[96]

92 Marriage certificate of Oliver Style and Harriett Elkington.

93 See *Brown Boots in Earlsdon* by Mary Montes (Coventry and Warwickshire Historical Association Pamphlet No. 15).

94 Birth certificate of Harriett Elkington, registered 22nd September 1845.

95 1833-1892. James Elkington started work as a silk ribbon weaver, but by 1874 had forged a career as a taxidermist as well as picture framing, placing adverts in local newspapers. See, for example, *Coventry Times*, 30th April 1879. He married Emma Inwood in 1861.

96 Born 1834.

Thomas,[97] Sarah Ann,[98] Selina[99] and Elizabeth.[100] Ann,[101] Walter[102] and Amelia[103] joined them in the years that followed.

At the time of the 1861 census, when Harriett was fifteen, she was living at 16 White Friars Lane and working as a silk cleaner.[104]

Now, three years later at St Thomas's, as the twenty-two year old groom stood in front of the Rev Frederick Gough he declared his middle name as 'Cromwell' – thus appearing on the marriage certificate as the grand-sounding 'Oliver Cromwell Style'.[105] He was recorded as a watch finisher living at Union Street,[106] off the Butts, his father John also a watch finisher.

Harriett, the nineteen year old bride, was a weaver, also living on Union Street. Her father was Thomas Elkington, also a weaver.

It was the classic union of the two main industries in Coventry at the time.

In front of witnesses William Style – Oliver's elder brother – and his wife Charlotte,[107] Harriett signed her name while Oliver made his mark, indicating that he was unable to write.[108]

*

Having completed his apprenticeship, and now able to consider himself a fully-fledged craftsman, Oliver set about earning a living

97 1837-1901. A butcher, who moved to Wales in the 1870s. He married Mary Griffin in 1858.

98 Born 1839. Married Abraham Turner, a watchmaker, in 1867.

99 Born 1841. Married Henry Turner, a watchmaker, in March 1861.

100 1843-1921. Married Samuel Evans, an engraver, in February 1867.

101 1847-1932. Married Alfred North, a watchmaker, in March 1868.

102 1850-1941. Starting work as a ribbon weaver, Walter became a successful coal merchant. He married Selina Gilbert in 1870.

103 Born and died 1852.

104 1861 census.

105 There is no official record of Oliver being blessed with the name 'Cromwell', apart from on the birth certificates or baptismal registers for his children, which he no doubt told the registrar himself.

106 Union Street is now Windsor Street. Although the road follows the same line, none of the original buildings remain.

107 William Style and Charlotte Wright had married less than a year earlier, on 26th September 1863.

108 Information from marriage certificate of Oliver Style and Harriett Elkington, 1st August 1864.

for his new family.

A watchmaker would sometimes work at home, especially if the premises had a 'topshop' – an airy room on the upper floor whose enormous windows allowed for maximum light by which the watchmakers would work, as the weavers had done before them – but if not he would rent a 'sitting' from a neighbour of a few shillings a week.[109]

After the wedding Oliver began renting a chair from a watchmaker named Abraham Knight, who had a workshop nearby on the Butts.[110] It did not take long for Oliver's temper to get the better of him, and when an altercation arose in November he found himself again before the magistrates, charged with violently assaulting Knight. Newspaper coverage included an insight into the way a watch finisher worked at the premises of others:

> "Abraham Knight said: 'I am a watch finisher, living in the Butts. The defendant occupies a seat in my shop. On the day the assault was committed a dispute arose between us as to some work which I refused to give up till it was paid for. As a consequence of this, the defendant was most abusive during the whole day, and threatened me repeatedly. About half-past four o'clock in the afternoon I sent for a policeman to have him turned out of my house. Before the police arrived he went to light his gas to continue his work. I refused to let him go on any longer, and put my hand upon the top of the gas to put it out, when the defendant threatened me if I did it. I put the gas out, when he attacked me in the most violent manner, and in the struggle my legs got entangled in the legs of a chair, and occasioned me to fall upon the floor, by which my arm was broken in two places. While I was upon the floor the defendant continued to strike and kick me, and afterwards got a hammer to strike me, but my wife took it from him. I was so seriously injured that I was obliged to call in the aid of Mr Bicknell,[111] who set my arm and

109 See *Brown Boots in Earlsdon* by Mary Montes (Coventry and Warwickshire Historical Association Pamphlet No. 15).

110 No. 43, according to census returns. Abraham Knight was thirty-two at the time of this attack by Oliver Style, and had married Maria Ball in 1852 when he was twenty.

111 Dr Edward Bicknell of Union Street, who had attended Oliver's father John Style after he'd been stabbed back in 1848.

> described the injuries I had sustained.'
>
> Richard Jolly, a journeyman [watchmaker] working in the same shop, and the apprentice of the complainant, both corroborated his statement.
>
> Style, in his defence, said: 'One of my masters had complained of the polishing of his work by the apprentice of the complainant, and I remonstrated with him about it. In consequence of this disagreement he refused to give me up some polished works which the apprentice had done for me. I tried to induce the complainant to let me have the work to go on with, as my employer had sent for the watches I had in hand, but he said he would not till I had paid for it. The complainant was the first to commence the quarrel, by putting out my gas and threatening to throw me downstairs.'
>
> The defendant's brother [William] was called, and said: 'On Tuesday last I had occasion to call at Mr Knight's. When I got there I found the complainant and the defendant struggling together. Knight had something in his hand, which I believe was a hammer. I also heard him call out to his wife to bring his gun that he might shoot the defendant.'"

Commenting on the severity of the offence, the Bench fined Oliver £5, with the threat of a two month prison sentence if he failed to pay up.[112]

The incident – and certain loss of work – stayed with Oliver Style for a long, long time.

In the early hours of Tuesday, 24th May 1870 – more than five years later – he was walking along Spon Street with a group of friends having enjoyed a night out, when he saw Abraham Knight ahead of him. Running towards him, he started abusing the older man, saying "There is an old grievance between you and me; pull off your coat, and let us have a turn or two."

Police Constable Carr happened to be on duty nearby, standing beside the Punch Bowl public house,[113] when he saw the mob

112 *Coventry Standard*, 26th November 1864.

113 Opened before 1774 at 104 Spon End, the Punch Bowl closed in 1911. The location is currently occupied by Rainbow Dragon, a Chinese takeaway.

The Punch Bowl, to the left of the crowd standing under the canopy, where PC Carr saw Oliver Style harassing Abraham Knight.

harassing Knight. As he arrested Style, one of the crowd, a young man named John Christian, attempted to rescue his friend by grabbing him and trying to pull him away. PC Carr took a statement from Knight, who had sought sanctuary in the Shamrock tavern,[114] and at the magistrates' hearing both Style and Christian received fines of 5s with costs.[115]

It might appear that Abraham Knight was an unwilling victim. But in truth, he seems to have been an odious character.

Six months after his close shave with Oliver Style and the drunken gang on Spon End, he found himself summoned to appear in court by his apprentice, a young man named John Sidwell, after Knight had complained about his work before violently assaulting him

114 No. 42 Sherbourne Street, on its northern corner with Upper Spon Street. The Shamrock closed in 1908.

115 *Coventry Herald*, 27th May 1870.

and threatening to throw him down the stairs. Sensing a fine - or worse, a custodial sentence – Knight turned the tables by issuing a summons against Sidwell, complaining of 'bad conduct' by the apprentice. The magistrates allowed them to settle the case by mutual consent.[116]

In July 1872 Knight made a complaint to magistrates against another watch finisher, William Palmer, saying that the two were neighbours on the Butts and one afternoon the latter had come home drunk and threatened to inflict bodily harm on Knight if he got hold of him; in his defence, Palmer told the Bench that while he didn't deny the drunken threat, Knight had been spreading malicious rumours, saying that William mistreated and starved his children.[117] The magistrates took this into account and bound him over to keep the peace for three months.[118]

Six months later, in January 1873, Knight was seen beating his wife in Union Street, with blood running freely from her wounds. A watch jeweller named John Asplin,[119] who knew him, approached and said, "Abraham, don't." For his trouble he was warned by Knight that he would "knock his ——— head off."

Nearby was Knight's sister-in-law, who asked Mr Asplin to protect her from the violence. Standing in front of her and, acting as a shield, the jeweller was punched several times in the face and kicked, all the while having his life verbally threatened by Abraham

116 *Coventry Standard*, 2nd December 1870.

117 The census of the previous year records thirty year old William Palmer living at 40 the Butts with wife Elizabeth and their three children, along with apprentice Joseph Hill. In 1881 they were at the same address, but by now the number of offspring had risen to six. In fact, William Palmer and his family lived at 40 the Butts until his death in 1908, raising a family of eight children in total. He left £723 to his family – some £60,000 today. This does not sound like a man who mistreated his children.

118 *Coventry Herald*, 26th July 1872.

119 At the time of this incident John Asplin was thirty-two years old, living at 46 Union Street with his family, then consisting of wife Louisa and children Charles, Elizabeth, John Jr and Louisa Jr. Three further sons – James, Herbert and Albert – would join the family in the years that followed.

Sovereign Place.

Knight.[120]

In April 1874 Knight was charged with disorderly conduct in Sovereign Place,[121] and in September 1875 appeared in court having summoned a neighbouring watchmaker named David Spencer,[122] who had wandered home drunk and stood underneath Knight's window at two in the morning, challenging him to a fight. Knight complained that Spencer had frequently annoyed him over the past couple of years. Knowing him a little better, however, perhaps a

120 *Coventry Herald*, 3rd January 1873.

121 *Coventry Standard*, 1st May 1874

122 Fifty-one year old David Spencer lived at 47 the Butts with wife Sarah and their daughter Sarah Jr, an unmarried twenty-nine year old described in the 1871 census as an 'imbecile', and her illegitimate son Charles, aged seven. The *Coventry Standard* of 9th May 1868 reported that one John Gutteridge, who had been adjudged by magistrates to be the boy's father, had been sentenced to three months' imprisonment for non-payment of maintenance towards the child's upkeep. Sarah Spencer died in January 1874 [*Coventry Standard*, 9th January 1874]. Her parents appear to have done a fine job of raising their grandson; Charles became a watch finisher, no doubt learning the skill from grandfather David, and married Eliza Hogan on Christmas Day 1889.

glimmer of the truth in this case came when David Spencer said in his defence that Knight had previously threatened him, and 'showed him' a knife.[123]

But the truest portrayal of Abraham Knight's personality was perhaps revealed on his father's death, in April 1876.

Thomas Knight, also a watchmaker, had been a recipient of the Freeman's Seniority Fund, thereby receiving a form of pension. He seems to have been well respected before his death, which appeared to have been caused by an overdose of the laudanum lacing his rum.

The *Coventry Herald*, covering the inquest held at the Spread Eagle on West Orchard Street, reported:

> "Abraham Knight, watch finisher, Broomfield Place, said: 'Deceased was my father. He was seventy-one years of age, and had been a habitual drunkard for many years. I last saw him alive about three weeks ago at half-past ten at night. He was not sober then. Last night I was sent for to [go to] him at about seven o'clock, but I did not go. The man who came to me told me he was dying, having taken fourpenny worth of laudanum in some rum. At about half-past ten the same messenger came again, and told me he was dead. He told me the deceased was very drunk on Saturday night. The reason I did not go —.'
>
> The Coroner: 'We don't want any reason. The reason is palpable enough.'
>
> The Foreman: 'From want of feeling, I should think.'
>
> The Coroner: 'Exactly so.
>
> (To the Witness): You may go."[124]

So much for the camaraderie of some members of the close-knit watchmaking community.[125]

123 *Coventry Herald*, 17th September 1875.

124 *Coventry Herald*, 14th April 1876.

125 Abraham Knight married Maria Ball at St John the Baptist on 2nd February 1852, and the couple went on to have four children. According to a report in the *Coventry Herald* of 3rd October 1879, Maria had left her husband by that time, and he had taken to watching her new abode in the hope of catching her with another man. On this occasion he did – a neighbour – who Knight attacked so severely that he was unconscious for seven hours. Abraham Knight died in 1909 aged seventy-five, no doubt few lamenting his passing.

*

All this was still to come. At some point after the alleged assault of Knight, Oliver and Harriett moved from Union Street to Thomas Street, the entrance to which was opposite the church where they married, across the Butts.[126] On 22nd February 1865 – just six months after the happy event – they welcomed their first child, daughter Edith Annie. Harriett gave birth at her parents' home at 16 White Friars Lane.[127] She was baptised at St Thomas's ten months later, on 24th December 1865.[128]

A brother soon followed, when Oliver Thomas Style was born on 21st January 1867.[129] Soon after the family moved from Thomas Street to 84 Craven Street,[130] in the heart of the Chapel Fields district which had been created twenty years earlier specifically for those engaged in the watchmaking trade.

While watchmaking was undertaken all over Coventry, because of the need to be in close proximity to others working on the next part of a watch's production, those engaged in the trade tended to congregate in the Spon Street, Spon End and Butts Lane areas, to the west of the city. But as the industry boomed, the already overcrowded courts became unbearable.

There was limited scope for expansion due to the protected Lammas and Michaelmas lands bordering the city, so it was a boon when a twenty-acre area of land west of Spon End, which was owned by the Sir Thomas White Charity, became available.[131]

126 Address taken from baptismal register for Edith Annie Style.
127 Midwife's Register, courtesy Pat Style; Style family Bible.
128 Baptismal register for Edith Annie Style.
129 Birth certificate of Oliver Thomas Style, registered 2nd February 1867.
130 Various birth and death certificates; 1871 census.
131 Sir Thomas White was Lord Mayor of London in 1553. A great philanthropist, he founded the charity in his name in 1542, which still exists today. White gifted £1,400 (£500,000 today) to the Coventry Corporation in order that they could purchase land, on the condition that a portion of the income from it be used to give interest-free loans to apprentices in Coventry, enabling them to set up in business. The fact that Hill, Olorenshaw and Marriott intended to build a community for a burgeoning Coventry trade would have made the decision to sell easier for the Corporation.

Lord Street, Chapel Fields.

It was purchased in 1846 for £3,751[132] by watchmakers Joseph Olorenshaw and William Hill, along with builder James Marriott.[133]

The land had been the location in the twelfth century for a lazar house – an isolation site for lepers positioned at a remote distance from the city, as it had been at the time. The centre of the colony was the Chapel of St Mary Magdalene, believed to have been a sister of the Biblical leper Lazarus.[134]

A plan for the new community – named Chapel Fields[135] in remembrance of the land's original use – was soon drawn up.

132 Around £250,000 today.

133 *The Coventry We Have Lost: Earlsdon and Chapelfields Explored* (2011) by David Fry and Albert Smith.

134 The remains of the chapel were discovered in the twentieth century in the grounds of what is now the Four Provinces Club, at the north end of Craven Street where it meets Allesley Old Road. See *The Coventry We Have Lost: Earlsdon and Chapelfields Explored* (2011) by David Fry and Albert Smith (2011).

135 Although now known by its single word name, Chapelfields, the district was called Chapel Fields until the twentieth century. With the events of this book taking place before that time, I have retained the two-word spelling.

Comprising a triangular area bordered by the Birmingham Turnpike Road[136] to the north and Hearsall Common to the south, Craven Street was constructed with Mount Street, Lord Street and Duke Street running off it. Some two hundred plots were available, and within five years seventy houses had been built and occupied. Of these, eighty-two men were engaged in the watchmaking trade and only nine in other occupations.[137]

Because each man might have different skill within the 'production line', Chapel Fields became a watchmaking 'factory'. A trade directory of the 1850s shows a Mr Austin, a springer, living at No. 1 Craven Street, while Mr Southam, a watch jeweller, lived next door. Ebenezer Player, an enamel dial painter, was at No. 6, and an escapement maker named Radburn lived at No. 38.[138] Others in the same streets offered case making, glass cutting and watch finishing. Their children would also be involved, the youngest as errand boys taking a watch to the next man along the street to add his part, and others as apprentices.

To serve the new community shops began to open, and in 1860 an offshoot of the Methodist Church on Queen's Road opened on Lord Street.[139] It was not long before a raft of public houses opened their doors: the Coombe Abbey on Craven Street was first, in 1850,[140] followed by the Nursery Gardens[141] on Lord Street two years later. Others soon followed: the New Inn (now the Chestnut

136 Now the Allesley Old Road.

137 1851 census. See also *Moments in Time: The History of the Coventry Watch Industry Volume 1* by the Coventry Watch Museum Project Limited (5th Edition: 2014).

138 Information from *The Coventry Watchmakers' Heritage Trail: A Guided Walk Through the Watchmaking Areas of Spon End and Chapelfields in Coventry* by the Coventry Watch Museum Project Limited (3rd Revised Edition: 2014). Much of Chapel Fields still exists, and certain houses have blue plaques upon their walls to indicate their significance to the watch making industry. The booklet *The Coventry Watchmakers' Heritage Trail* guides the reader to each of these, and gives detailed information. Put together by the knowledgeable Coventry Watch Museum Project, it is a wonderful guide.

139 *Moments in Time: The History of the Coventry Watch Industry Volume 1* by the Coventry Watch Museum Project Limited (5th Edition: 2014).

140 Finally closed in 2017 after 167 years.

141 Now the Nursery Tavern.

Craven Street, with the Coombe Abbey extreme right.

Tree), the Craven Arms, the Hearsall Inn and others opened their doors to the thirsty community, and the watchmaker's day to day business took place within their walls.

With their smart front and longer rear gardens, the houses of Chapel Fields must have seemed a world away from the cramped courts of Spon Street and the inner city Gosford Street workshops where the watchmakers had previously struggled to ply their trade.

While several of the properties had large, light and airy topshops constructed, these were always at the rear to maintain the respectable street-side appearance of the community.

But despite providing a more genteel environment compared to the Butts and Spon Street, Chapel Fields still saw its share of wrongdoing. A fortnight before Oliver Jr was born, a young man named James Thompson was in court, charged with stealing items relating to his employment at the premises of a Mr Sanderson, a watchmaker on Craven Street,[142] and the previous year eleven year old Thomas Sterland was accused of stealing twelve shillings from the till of Mr Henry Keene, another watchmaker who lived at No.

142 *Coventry Herald*, 4th January 1867.

74.[143]

PC Green was on duty in Craven Street at midnight one Saturday when he saw Joseph Parker lying on the ground, insensible after evidently enjoying a night in one or more of the street's hostelries. The constable helped him to his feet, but Parker refused to go home and instead challenged the officer to a fight. He was taken to the cells to sleep off his bravado.[144]

Nonetheless, these must have been very happy times for Oliver and Harriett; they had a son to add to their daughter Edith, and the young family were living in the heart of the watchmaking community, with Oliver no doubt picking up a lot of work.

But, just as they dared to look to the future, tragedy struck. Daughter Edith, just three-and-a-half years old, died at the family home after suffering for three weeks with *scarlatina maligna*, the same affliction which had claimed Oliver's brother Henry back in 1855.[145]

The terrible nature of the disease was described in detail by Dr A. Myers, the Assistant-Surgeon to the Coldstream Guards, in an article published in the *British Medical Journal* earlier that same year. It gives a stark insight into the horrors suffered by poor little Edith:

> "A boy, aged 3 years and 3 months, previously healthy, excepting that he had a mild attack of measles in December, awoke at

143 *Coventry Herald*, 5th October 1866. Address and forename from 1871 census.

144 *Coventry Standard*, 25th March 1864. Earlier unsavoury incidents in Craven Street include the inquest held at the New Inn (now the Chestnut) in July 1862 into the death of Ann Flanders, who lived on Mount Street with her husband and young family, and drowned herself in a water butt while gripped in a severe depression (*Coventry Standard*, 18th July 1862); a charge of corruption against Superintendent Skermer of Coventry's police and one of his detectives, with one Joseph White, a watchmaker of 23 Craven Street involved (*Coventry Standard*, 10th June 1859); and PC Quinsey, on duty on Craven Street in the early hours, witnessing a bankrupt watchmaker and his wife emptying their house of furniture between midnight and two in the morning to reduce the value of their assets (*Coventry Herald*, 27th July 1861).

145 Death certificate of Edith Annie Style, registered 3rd August 1868. During her final three days Edith had also suffered from uremia.

> 1.00am on January 6th, complained of sickness, and vomited several times until 7.00am, when he was slightly convulsed. At 11.00am, when first seen by me, he was slightly feverish, with quick pulse; his skin was rather hot; the tongue coated with a brownish fur on each side of the median line and red towards the margins; and a faint blush was observed over the front of the chest, with a few scattered papillæ. Castor oil and a warm bath were ordered; the former acted freely in a short time. At 3.00pm, immediately after the bath, he had a violent attack of convulsions which lasted nearly half an hour; and during that time, he became, according to his mother's account, quite black, foamed at the mouth, and was momentarily expected to die. After the attack subsided, he continued quite delirious and more or less convulsed until 1.00am on January 7th, when he asked a few questions rationally, and had a good voluntary evacuation from the bowels and bladder; the faeces was very dark and offensive.
>
> At 11.00am, he was seen again by me, another surgeon having been in attendance in the meantime, when the delirium was extreme; the tongue, dry and brown, was protruded to its utmost and rolled from side to side; the eyeballs were deeply suffused, the straight arteries being more especially prominent; the pupils were contracted to the finest point; there was no squinting. The skin was hot and dry, but there was no appearance of eruption over any part, nor swelling of the throat. The pulse was very rapid, and felt with difficulty. Such continued to be his condition until 7.00pm, when death occurred; excepting that the mother remarked that he became gradually cold from the feet upwards (in her own words, "died upwards"), and immediately after death the body became rapidly livid in the same direction."[146]

The loss of little Edith was reported the same day by grieving mother Harriett, who had been present at the death. The sudden illness and death of their eldest child would obviously have deeply affected Oliver and Harriett, and it is believed that a braided lock of light-brown hair tied with a purple ribbon, found pressed between the pages of the family Bible decades later, was snipped from Edith's head as a memento.[147]

146 *British Medical Journal*, Vol. 1, No. 370 (February 1, 1868), p. 97.
147 Courtesy Alison Kukla.

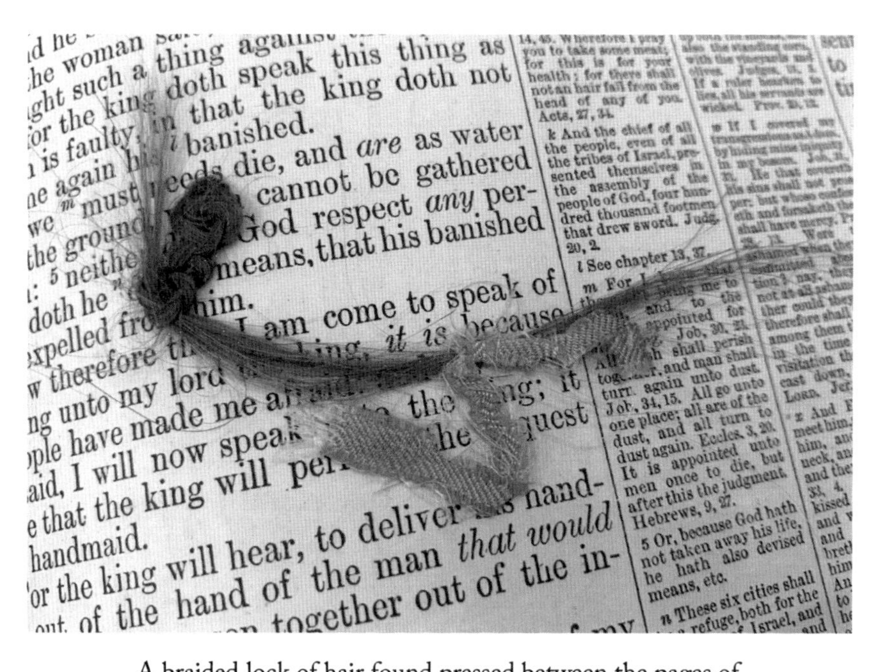

A braided lock of hair found pressed between the pages of the Style family Bible, believed to have been snipped from Edith's head.

As if things weren't stressful enough, Harriett was at this time pregnant again. It's not known whether the baby arrived early due to worry, but thankfully another daughter was born without any problems on 30th November 1868.[148] In the Victorian tradition, they named her Edith Harriett after her recently-departed sister.

The family continued to grow. On 27th November 1870 another daughter, Elizabeth Jane, was born,[149] followed by Rhoda on 15th June 1872.[150] A son, Herbert James, became the ultimate present when he arrived on Christmas Day 1873.[151]

With the growing family, Oliver desperately needed to not only maintain his workload, but to increase it if possible. This may have worked for a time, but eventually the pressure caught up with him.

On 11th March 1874 he appeared before magistrates at

148 Date of birth from 1939 England and Wales Register; Style family Bible.
149 Birth certificate of Elizabeh Jane Style.
150 Dates of birth recorded on baptismal register; Style family Bible.
151 Style family Bible.

Birmingham charged with breach of contract by the local watch manufacturing company Barnett Brothers, who had a premises on Vittoria Street.

Oliver had promised to finish a number of watches for the firm, and despite an earlier court appearance where he was ordered to complete the work within a fortnight he had yet to do so. Barnett Bros had lost £15 as a result of his tardiness. The magistrates ordered him to cover the £15 loss, and also the court costs.[152]

*

At the very end of the following year – 30th December 1875 – Oliver and Harriett's fourth and final daughter, Florence, was born. She was baptised five weeks later, on 6th February 1876, at All Saints on Far Gosford Street, just around the corner from the family home on Harnall Row. Intriguingly, Rhoda and Herbert were also baptised there at the same time;[153] was it a case of the location of All Saint's being conveniently located, or was there a guilty secret which had recently come to light which resulted in Oliver wanting to be seen as a good father?

Just two months later, on 12th April, he appeared at Coventry Police Court before Magistrates Dewes, Pears and Carter charged with failing to maintain payments for an illegitimate child of which he was the father. The names of mother and child have been lost in the mists of time, and there is no record even of when the child was born. But an order had been made upon him in the past, as he was summoned for being in arrears to the sum of £3 18s 6d.[154]

Informing the magistrates that as he was unable to find the money without more time, he assumed it meant he must go to prison. The

152 *Birmingham Daily Post*, 12th March 1874.

153 Church of England Baptisms, 1813-1910: Coventry, All Saints, 1875-1899.

154 As the common weekly order imposed at the time was in the region of 2s 6d, this puts Oliver at around thirty-six weeks in the arrears, so unless he kept up initial payments only to lapse with his payments, the order would have been made around July 1875. The child was therefore probably born after Rhoda and before Florence, his daughters with wife Harriett.

magistrates agreed, but warned him that he would still be liable for the debt on his release. As he was sentenced to three months' imprisonment, Oliver commented: "If I can't pay now, I can't pay when I come out."[155]

Whether Harriett was aware of her husband's liaison with another woman is unknown. But barely five months after his release from prison they were bound together in tragedy yet again, when their daughter Rhoda died at the family home of 1 Harnall Row after suffering with scarlatina for two months, passing away on 2nd January 1877. Her father registered the sad event that same day.[156]

To confirm their reunion, another son, Arthur Edward Style, was born on 1st December at Harnall Row to see out 1877 in a happier mood. Once again, his father gave his name to the registrar as Oliver 'Cromwell' Style.[157]

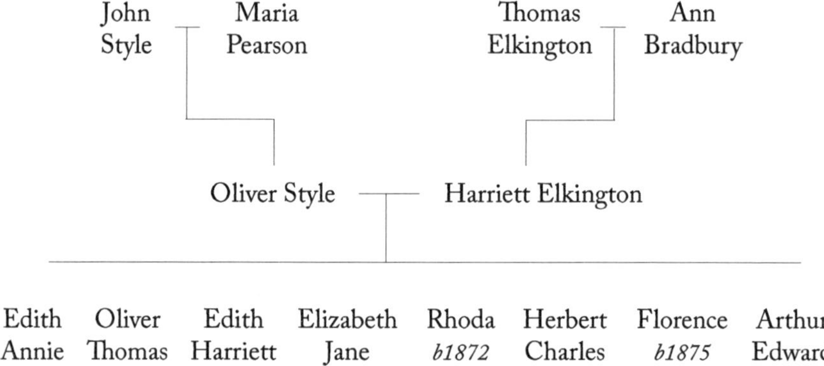

155 *Kenilworth Advertiser*, 22nd April 1876.
156 Death certificate of Rhoda Style, registered 2nd January 1877.
157 Birth certificate of Arthur Edward Style, registered 8th January 1878.

4.

"NOW I'VE GOT MY REVENGE"

By the turn of the 1880s the Style family was complete. The birth of Arthur offered the chance for Oliver and Harriett to try to move on from the loss of Rhoda, and they probably looked to the new decade with some optimism.

But a tragic local incident in the Spring of 1880 would have acted as a reminder that fate was always ready to deal a cruel blow.

On 16th March that year a cabman named John Bethel was leading his horse along Spon End when he stopped outside the Malt Shovel public house.[158] Deciding to stop for a while – and no doubt a refreshment – he instructed two young boys nearby to get into the cart and continue on the route, which the horse apparently knew well. They were so small that they couldn't see the road in front of them, so they sat on some bags in order to gain a slightly loftier vantage point, with eleven year old Amos Woodward[159] taking the reins.

The cart trundled off, passing under the Spon End railway arches, and soon turned left into Craven Street, with the old horse[160]

158 According to historiccoventry.co.uk, a pint was first pulled at the Malt Shovel from at least 1800. It closed its doors in 2011.

159 The name of the second boy in the cart is not recorded in newspaper reports. Amos Woodward was born on 24th August 1868. He married Emily Adder on 22nd October 1894, and retired from his work as a tinsmith's labourer to New Street, Coventry. He died in 1944.

160 Mr Bethel later told the coroner at the inquest that the horse was twenty-six years old, and he'd owned it for sixteen.

The Craven Arms, bearing the name of the landlord, F.H. Smith.
His son William was killed in the street in the foreground.

plodding along at a steady pace.[161]

Ahead of them, by the Craven Arms tavern, were a group of small boys collecting horse manure from the dirt road with buckets and spades.

With the two juvenile drivers so low on the cart they were unable to see how close the horse was to the group, and so continued on their journey. As they approached the older lads jumped out of the way, but the smallest, three year old William Smith, fell and was struck on the head by the horse's hooves, being immediately rendered insensible. He was carried to the Craven Arms, where his father, Frederick Smith, was the landlord.[162]

161 Although not mentioned in newspaper reports of the incident, it seems likely that Mr Bethel was delivering to pubs of the area, having stopped at the Malt Shovel and knowing his horse would know the route to Craven Street, which had several taverns.

162 Although records show Frederick Henry Smith to have only recently taken over at the Craven Arms at the time of his son's death, he would continue as the landlord there until his own passing in 1910. He had previously worked as a watch jeweller, living at 64 Craven Street, next door to the tavern. [Census returns and Trade Directory].

Poor William lingered for almost a week, never regaining consciousness, and passed away on 22nd March. An inquest held at the Coventry and Warwickshire Hospital the following day heard Dr Aitken's painful evidence as to the cause of death:

> "...a large scalp wound and general injury to the whole face... There was no fracture of the skull, but the bone was greatly bruised. The direct cause of death was inflammation of the brain and convulsions."[163]

After the jury returned a verdict of Accidental Death, Coroner Mr Dewes[164] left those present in no doubt as to what he thought of the conduct of Bethel by leaving the horse and cart in the care of the two young boys, but the only punishment he could exact was to withhold the cabman's expenses. It was, as can be imagined, scant solace for Frederick Smith and his family.

Had the Style family still been living on Craven Street, with their own experiences of losing a child so young there's no doubt that Oliver and Harriett would have offered some words of consolation for the Smith family. But they had long returned to Harnall Row, and Oliver's problems were about to get much worse.

*

Relations between Oliver and Harriett had been strained for quite a while – Harriett would later say that they "had been on unhappy terms for a long time."[165] In May 1879 the couple had been at the Old Half Moon on Hertford Place, a tavern popular with the watchmaking community which was run by a young widow named Maria Feltham.

Once again an argument ensued between the couple, and Oliver

163 'Sad Accident in Coventry'. *Kenilworth Advertiser*, 27th March 1880.

164 Solicitor Thomas Dewes of Hay Lane, Coventry was the Coroner for North Warwickshire for sixteen years between 1866 and his death in January 1882, when the position was taken by Charles Iliffe. See the *Atherstone, Nuneaton and Warwickshire Times* of 7th January 1882 for a full account of Dewes' illustrious career.

165 Testimony of Harriett Style, *Coleshill Chronicle*, 10th July 1880.

accused Harriett of being too friendly with other men.[166] Two names cropped up: Henry White[167] and Walter Goddard.[168]

Oliver threatened his wife, picking up some measures to throw at her, then stormed out. Harriett went to her mother's house on Much Park Street, where she remained for a fortnight until her husband sent one of the children to ask her to come home.[169] They remained under the same roof for the best part of the following year, albeit a fractured existence with Oliver Style frequently abusing his wife.

Things came to a head on the evening of 27th April 1880, when together Harriett and Oliver attended the Liberal Ball, held at the Corn Exchange on Hertford Street.[170] Very soon they got into a

166 'Murderous Outrages in Coventry: The Prisoner Before The Magistrates'. *Coventry Times*, 7th July 1880.

167 Incorrectly named 'John' in some newspaper reports, William Henry White was born in January 1848 in Coventry, son of watch finisher William White and his wife Eliza. He went by the name 'Henry' to avoid confusion with his father. In January 1871 White married Elizabeth Pym, and the couple welcomed a son, Frederick, three months later. Daughter Ellen joined them in November 1872, and another son, Frank, was born two years later. Two more sons were born, for some unknown reason given almost the same name: Walter John (1876) and Walter Edwin (1878). At the time of the assault by Oliver Style, White was a thirty-two year old watch roller and lever maker living with his family at 19 Hertford Place, close to the Old Half Moon. He would certainly have known Harriett and Oliver Style. Sadly, wife Elizabeth died in January 1884, and son Walter Edwin passed away at just seven years old the following year. William White married again in July 1889, to the exotically-named Mahala Pym – the niece of his first wife Elizabeth, and eighteen years his junior. He died on 10th October 1918.

168 Well-known to Maria Feltham was Walter Goddard, a watchmaker who had in 1861 lodged with her future husband's family at 12 Hertford Square while a single man. At the time of Maria's troubles with Oliver Style, Walter Goddard was thirty-eight years old and married with a young family of four children. They were living at 3 Hertford Square, and Walter therefore certainly used the Old Half Moon. Goddard continued his work as a watch maker, moving first to 3 Chapel Yard, Spon Street [1901 census] and then 4 Broomfield Place [1911]. He died in 1918.

169 'Murderous Outrages in Coventry: The Prisoner Before The Magistrates'. *Coventry Times*, 7th July 1880.

170 *Coventry Times*, 25th February 1880. The Coventry Corn Exchange opened in March 1856, to be used in the main for concerts and lectures. Charles Dickens appeared there the following December. In the early Twentieth century it was screening films, and was renamed the Empire in 1914.

row because a friend of Harriett's – almost certainly Maria Feltham – had told her that Oliver had been "treating a woman to port wine" on the day their child had died.[171] When Oliver complained that it was a lie, Harriett responded that she had known what time he'd left work on the day in question, and what time he had arrived home, inferring there was ample opportunity for him to get up to no good.

Mrs Feltham arrived at the Ball, and a frosty conversation passed between Oliver and Harriett. When his wife stopped to talk to an old schoolfriend, Oliver took the opportunity to turn round and punch Mr White in the face. Harriett looked over and saw a Mrs Ward holding her hand to her bleeding nose, inadvertently struck by Oliver in his attempt to hit White. Style apologised, and claimed that White had digged him in the ribs with his elbow, provoking the response.

Harriett had had enough; she gathered her things and went home.

The following Sunday, 2nd May, Maria Feltham arrived at the Styles' house with a young lady to discuss the rumours concerning Henry White – it was probably his wife, Elizabeth. Oliver complained about Mrs Feltham being at his house, and objected to Harriett going to the Old Half Moon; Maria said they could talk in the street.[172]

Called to appear before magistrates two days later, Oliver admitted striking White, but repeated the claim that he had been provoked. He was bound over, and ordered to pay two sureties of £5 each to keep the peace for three months.[173]

It was a relatively small penalty, but the latest incident in a long line of violence and petty jealousy, and the final straw for Harriett Style. Possibly following advice from Maria Feltham, the day after her husband's court appearance she left him.

*

171 Presumably Rhoda, who died on 2nd January 1877.

172 'Murderous Outrages in Coventry: The Prisoner Before The Magistrates'. *Coventry Times*, 7th July 1880.

173 *Coventry Times*, 12th May 1880.

Ironically, Maria Feltham had followed an identical path to Oliver Style.

She too had been born at one of London's watchmaking centres, in her case Islington, on 13th November 1846 to John Francis,[174] a watchmaker, who also relocated his family to Coventry and the new watchmaking community on Craven Street[175] when she was young.

By 1861 John Francis had died, and his widow Sarah and their children were living at 6 Hearsall Lane.[176]

At some point over the next five years Maria met Joseph Feltham, a young watchmaker living at Hertford Square off Albion Street.[177] The couple married at St Thomas's on 26th August 1866, two years after Oliver and Harriett Style had made their vows at the same altar. The groom was twenty-one, his bride nineteen.[178] Why the rush? Their daughter Sarah Elizabeth Feltham was born two months later, and baptised at St Thomas's on 3rd March 1867.[179] A son, Joseph Jr, followed in April 1869, and the family were back at St Thomas's that October for his own baptism.[180]

By this time Joseph Sr had taken over as landlord of the Old Half Moon,[181] situated on Hertford Place, at No. 27. The rear of this tavern created the southern border of Hertford Square, which was populated by families engaged in the watchmaking trade and had topshops on both sides. As two passageways allowed access to Hertford Place from the square, there's little doubt that Joseph, and his friends and neighbours, would have frequented the inn for several years. In this way the Old Half Moon became the place to drink for those engaged in the industry, with deals probably being struck on the premises most nights.

174 Baptismal register of Maria Elizabeth Francis.
175 1851 census.
176 1861 census.
177 1861 census and marriage certificate.
178 Marriage certificate.
179 Baptismal register of Sarah Elizabeth Feltham.
180 Baptismal register of Joseph Eaton Feltham.
181 *Kelly's Directory of Warwickshire*, 1868.

Hertford Square, showing the topshops on the upper floors.
In the background can be seen the rear of the Old Half Moon, with the arched entrances to Hertford Place.

The Feltham family were still running the tavern when Joseph Sr died there on 11th December 1877, aged just thirty-three. He had suffered in agony for a full year with laryngeal phthisis, which causes ulcers on the larynx and eventually destroys the vocal chords, and towards the end results in the sufferer literally drowning in their own blood.[182] It was an horrific way for poor Joseph to go.

Continuing in the only job she knew, Maria – now thirty-one years old and with two young children – took over the licence. Also on Hertford Place were the Hen and Chickens, on the corner with Butts Lane,[183] and the Hertford Arms at No. 20.[184] But the proximity of Hertford Square made the Half Moon popular with the watchmaking community, and Oliver and Harriett Style were among the regulars.

182 Death certificate of Joseph Eaton Feltham, registered 11th December 1877.

183 Opened in 1835, the Hen and Chickens was briefly renamed the Fowl and Firkin in 1993. It is currently called the Aardvark.

184 Situated at 20 Hertford Place, the tavern opened in 1840. It closed in 1986.

The embarrassing scene at the Liberal Ball had been the final straw for Harriett. She had moved into her mother's at 23c Much Park Street with her youngest, two year old Arthur, and left Oliver at Harnall Row with the elder five children, ranging from thirteen years old to five.

Oliver Jr was sent to Much Park Street on several occasions over the following month to ask his mother to come home, but she refused given her husband's violence towards her. The boy's uncle, James Elkington, was asked to go and see Oliver Sr, but he wanted nothing to do with him. On Wednesday, 26th May the boy went again, this time to James Elkington's house further along Much Park Street, and saw his mother there, saying that she had no love for her children otherwise she would have gone home. His aunt Sarah – Harriett's sister – was there, and threatened him, saying, "Go to ——, you young ———; I'll kick your ——— if you ain't off." Oliver went home to his father.[185]

There's no doubt that, as much as she missed her children, Harriett feared for her life – scared enough to go to the Police station that day to seek advice from PC James Radburn[186] – and decided to stay at Much Park Street.[187]

Her continued refusal to return home sent her husband into a rage; one which just twenty-four hours later would erupt with devastating consequences.

*

The start of Thursday, 27th May 1880 was quiet enough. Harriett and young Arthur probably spent a peaceful morning, while her estranged husband busied himself with work, and made sure the children went to school. He remained at home until three o'clock.[188]

Between six and seven that evening Oliver arrived at the

185 *Kenilworth Advertiser*, 17th July 1880.

186 The 1881 census return shows twenty-seven year old James Radburn, a police constable, living at 40 Lower Nelson Street with his wife Emily.

187 Testimony of Harriett Style at the magistrates' heading, as reported in the *Coleshill Chronicle*, 10th July 1880.

188 *Coventry Times*, 2nd June 1880.

shop of Bland and Sons, a gunmakers at 41 Whittall Street in Birmingham.[189] There he asked Edwin Bland, one of the partners, to look at a revolver. He told Bland that he was going to America, "to shoot the blacks," and purchased a six-chambered revolver and a box of fifty cartridges. Bland would later state that the weapon had a range of thirty yards, and would be accurate at around twenty.[190]

Now armed, and seething with rage, Oliver Style made his way back to Coventry, intent on getting his revenge on those who had conspired against him.

*

Supping in the Old Half Moon was William Veasey,[191] who had known Oliver by sight for two years. He saw him enter the inn at just after ten past nine.[192]

Approaching the bar, Oliver asked for a glass of ale. Maria

189 Testimony of Edwin Bland at the magistrates' hearing, as reported in the *Coleshill Chronicle*, 10th July 1880. Thomas Bland & Sons – of which twenty-three year old Edwin was one – were founded in 1840 in Birmingham and expanded to 106 Strand in London in 1872. The company continued at the Whittall Street address until the 1920s.

190 Testimony of Edwin Bland at the magistrates' hearing, as reported in the *Coleshill Chronicle*, 10th July 1880.

191 William John Veasey was born in 1855 at Whitechapel, east London. He was living in Coventry by the time of the 1871 census, and married Jane Howe at the city's St Michael's Church in January 1875. By the time of the shootings Veasey was working as a soda water maker, living on St John's Street. By now the family included three children. In February 1889 Veasey appeared before magistrates for not sending his eight-year-old son to school (presumably Henry Lewis Veasey, born in June 1880). The lad had instead been begging from door to door around the neighbourhood, and his father implored the magistrates to give him the birch, saying, "It's a rum thing to ask you to do, but I have beaten him to such an extent that the neighbours have threatened to summon me." (*Coventry Times*, Wednesday 20th February 1889). This came to pass three years later, when William Veasey was sentenced to a month's imprisonment for violently beating his son with a strap. The father's defence that he had told the boy to go out and sell cress, but instead he went and played football. He didn't intend to strike the boy's face with the strap, he said, thinking he had 'only' landed on his shoulders. The Chief Constable informed the magistrates that Veasey had continually assaulted his wife. William Veasey died in 1929 aged seventy-six.

192 Testimony of William Veasey. *Atherstone, Nuneaton and Warwickshire Times*, 17th July 1880.

Feltham, no doubt sick of the sight of him, refused. But her mother, Sarah Francis, came out of the parlour and drew the beer while Maria went out to the back part of the house.[193]

A watchmaker named James Pallett,[194] who lived at 5 Hertford Square,[195] had known Oliver for thirty years. He was in the tap room with nine or ten others, when his friend silently appeared in the doorway.[196] One of the group, James Styles,[197] another watchmaker living at 19 Hertford Place who had also known the newcomer for some time, called out "Hello Oliver, how are you?" but received no reply. Instead, Style went back out into the passage.

Suddenly, there was a loud report of a gun firing. William Veasey ran into the passage and saw Style standing there.[198] Lying on the floor was a man named Henry Jennings, who had been sitting on a stool in the tap room, opposite the door. He had been shot just above the knee.[199] Jennings would later say that Style, whom he had known for some time – and in fact had attended his court summons by Henry White two months earlier – had shouted "Someone must have it," as he fired the revolver through the tap room door.[200]

Veasey shouted, "You ——— fool, what are you doing?" Style

193 Testimony of Maria Feltham. *Atherstone, Nuneaton and Warwickshire Times*, 17th July 1880.

194 James Pallett was born to watchmaker Joseph and his wife Ann at Spon Street, being baptised on 23rd March 1838. The family remained in the house for many years, with James learning the watchmaking trade from his father. He married Harriet Cox in 1866, and the couple moved to Hertford Square where they raised a family of four daughters and two sons. Sadly one of them, Joseph, died in 1878 aged just ten years old.

195 1871 and 1881 census returns.

196 Testimony of James Pallett. *Atherstone, Nuneaton and Warwickshire Times*, 17th July 1880.

197 James Styles was born in 1848 in north London. He married Mary Ann Allen at St Thomas's, the watchmakers' church, on 18th February 1874.

198 Testimony of William Veasey. *Atherstone, Nuneaton and Warwickshire Times*, 17th July 1880.

199 Born in Coventry in 1846, Henry Jennings was by 1871 working as a baker, living at 15 Hertford Place with his wife Harriet and their two daughters, Sarah Ann and Rosanna. Another daughter, Alice, was born in 1874, but tragically Harriet died in March 1876 aged just twenty-four Henry grieved for two years before marrying Catherine Wallis, and by the time of the shooting the family were still living at 15 Hertford Place.

200 Testimony of Henry Jennings. *Coventry Times*, 30th June 1880.

responded, "Stand back, I am going to riddle the ———"[201]

James Pallett, on hearing the shot and seeing Jennings fall to the floor, walked towards the door and pushed it open.[202]

On hearing the door creak open Style turned round and took aim.[203] Hidden by the frame, Pallett saw a revolver pointing at his chest but not who had hold of it. He just had time to put his left hand up to protect himself when Style pulled the trigger; the bullet passed through the ball of his thumb and cut the collar of his waistcoat, coming to rest against a handkerchief tucked into the garment. Pallett staggered back onto the fender – it was a miracle he had not been killed.[204]

Veasey tried in vain to wrestle the revolver out of Style's hand, instead grabbing both hand and weapon, and the gunman was able to escape to the entrance to the parlour.[205] Not unreasonably, the inhabitants of the tap room closed and fastened the door.[206]

Maria Feltham, meanwhile, had heard the shots and made her way back into the parlour. It was the worst possible timing. As William Veasey stood with Styles, the gunman saw his nemesis framed into the doorway and shot her in the back. Veasey would later breathlessly tell the magistrates that he "felt the whizz of the bullet go by [my] arm and saw the flash go by [my] eyes." As Mrs Feltham screamed and fell, Veasey was able to catch her and help her to a chair.[207]

As the would-be murderer turned and escaped the tavern, leaving Bedlam behind him, Veasey followed. He caught up with him at the corner of the Poddy Croft,[208] at which point Style turned and asked why he was following him. Veasey said, "You are not going

201 Testimony of Veasey. *Atherstone, Nuneaton and Warwickshire Times*, 17th July 1880.
202 Testimony of James Pallett. *Coventry Times*, 2nd June 1880.
203 Testimony of Veasey. *Atherstone, Nuneaton and Warwickshire Times*, 17th July 1880.
204 Testimony of James Pallett. *Coventry Times*, 2nd June 1880.
205 Testimony of Veasey. *Atherstone, Nuneaton and Warwickshire Times*, 17th July 1880.
206 *Coventry Times*, 2nd June 1880.
207 Testimony of William Veasey. *Coventry Herald*, 9th July 1880.
208 Lammas land now roughly occupied by the Ikea store.

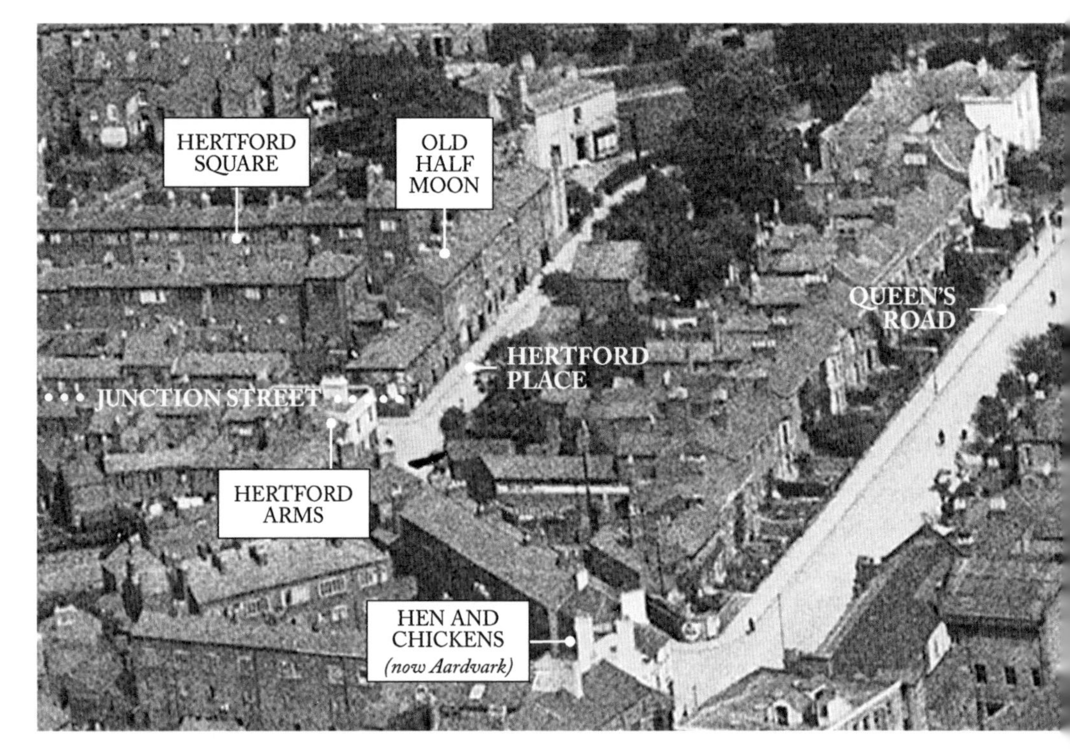

Aerial map of Coventry circa 1920 showing Hertford Place.
© Historic Environment Scotland

away like that," to which Style responded, ominously: "I have got two more left, and if you follow me you shall have them."

Wisely, Veasey stopped where he was and watched as the other man ran towards Stoneleigh Terrace and then Warwick Road, in the direction of Much Park Street.[209]

*

At her mother's house, at nine o'clock Harriett had put up the shutters and locked the door. Her hopes for a peaceful night were about to be rudely interrupted.

> "About half an hour afterwards a loud knock came to the door. My mother said, "Who is there?" The door was then bursted

209 Testimony of William Veasey. *Atherstone, Nuneaton and Warwickshire Times*, 17th July 1880.

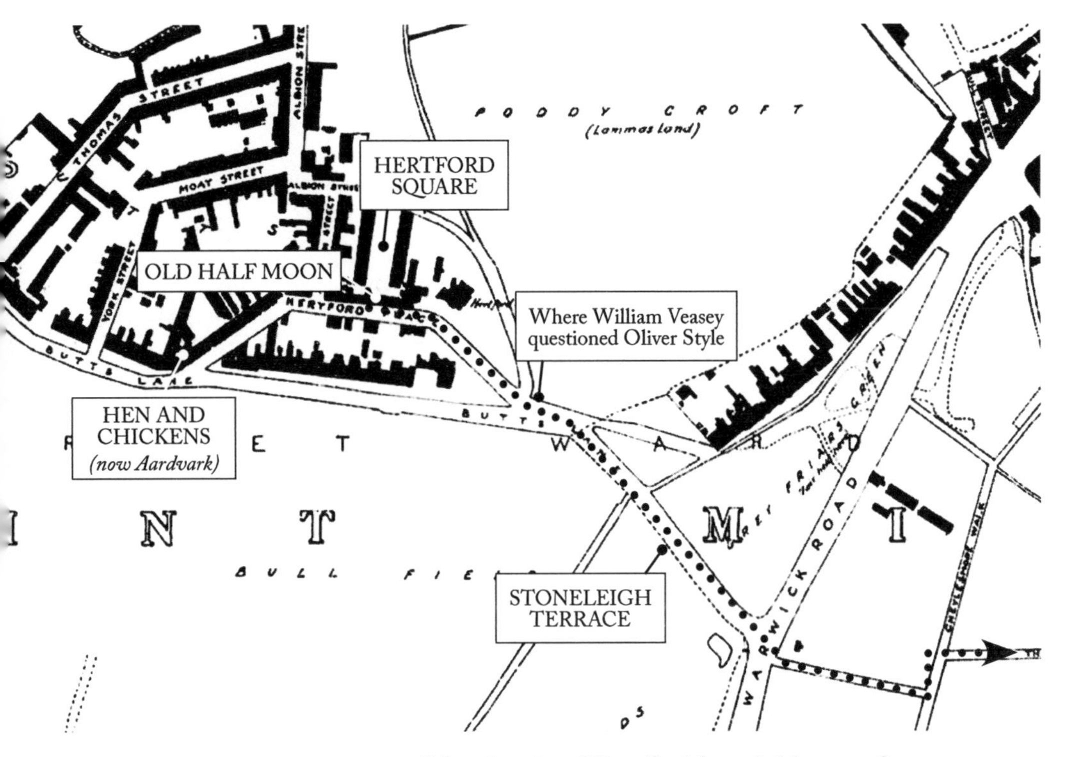

Map showing Oliver Style's probable route from the Old Half Moon towards Much Park Street.

open, and I saw my husband in the doorway, with one hand on the door and something in the other hand. He said, "Now I've got my revenge," and turning to my mother he said, "I will do for you, you old cow, first." He then lifted his hand up in the direction of my mother and fired what I thought was a pistol. When he had fired he said, "You're not done for yet," and fired a second time. My mother was then standing up.

He then turned round and fired at me. The child [Arthur, two-and-a-half] was in my arms at the time, and the shot struck me in the right shoulder.

He then caught hold of the hair of my head, and we wrestled out of doors together. We had got round the corner some ten yards from the door when he got me with my back to the wall and fired the pistol towards my heart. The pistol was not more than a foot from me when he fired. He fired with his right hand whilst he held me against the wall with his left. The shot struck the steel 'busk' in my stays and sent it into my flesh, and inflicted a

Much Park Street.

> wound just under the left breast.
>
> After he had fired [he] said, "There, that will do for you." I reeled against the wall, but did not fall.
>
> My thoughts came into my head, and I thought I would run to my brother's a little higher up the street. I don't know what became of [my husband] afterwards. I had the child in my arms all the time. I did not know that the child was hurt until I got to my brother's, when I found it was bleeding, the bullet having passed through the flesh of the forehead."[210]

In fact, as Harriett escaped to the safety of her brother James's house along Much Park Street at No. 90, Oliver Style was being apprehended by two men in the court at No. 23.

Living at No. 22, which joined No. 23 halfway up, was James Twigger.[211] From his bedroom window he could see anyone entering

210 Testimony of Harriett Style. *Coleshill Chronicle*, 10th July 1880.

211 Thirty-one year old James Twigger, a general labourer, lived at 22 Much Park Street with his wife Eliza. Living in the same court were his younger brother John and his family. While the 1881 census shows that Ann Elkington had moved to 20 Court 2 House Much Park Street following the shooting, at her old home were James and John Twigger's parents John and Elizabeth.

or leaving the Elkington house, and that evening he had retired to bed early but was not yet asleep when he heard a crash from next door. Getting out of bed and throwing open the window, he heard screaming and the sound of crockery being broken, and then the report of gunshots. Twigger saw Harriett coming out of the door, followed by her husband, who had hold of her as he said, "Ain't it done it, you ———, ain't it done it?" He then fired twice more.[212]

Living on the ground floor of No. 22 was Edward Davis. He also heard the shots, and put on his boots before going outside to investigate. He was just in time to see Harriett come around the corner carrying young Arthur in her arms, and Oliver catch up to her and fire again. As Davis approached Harriett made her escape. The labourer asked the crazed husband what he was doing – perhaps unnecessarily – and received the reply, "I have done what I intended to do, I have shot the ——— cat to the heart."

Style began walking down the yard, keeping the gun pointing at Davis, who followed him. Waiting at the other end was a man named William Carter, who had heard the commotion, and as Style walked backwards towards him he was able to grab his arms. At this Oliver threw the revolver into the air, saying, "I have done what I intended to do, you can take me."[213]

The two men kept a tight hold on him as they marched to the Police station on St Mary Street, where he was given into the custody of Constable Edwin Sale.[214]

It would be Oliver Style's last taste of freedom for more than two decades.

Hearing what Carter and Davis had to say, the officer charged Style with shooting his wife and mother-in-law with intent to murder. A search of the prisoner turned up the box of cartridges, of which thirty-eight were left, with four loose in his pocket. Eight shots had been fired in total.

The prisoner seemed excitable but sane, and gave officers at the

212 Testimony of James Twigger. *Coleshill Chronicle*, 10th July 1880.
213 Testimony of Edward Davis. *Coleshill Chronicle*, 10th July 1880.
214 Forename from 1881 census return, listing forty year old Police Constable Edwin Sale as living at 2 West Street with his wife and three children.

station a rational account of his actions, but commented, seemingly referring to Henry White: "I have been driven to it; but I have missed the right one."[215]

At 90 Much Park Street, James Elkington listened carefully to his sister's story, and after making sure she and Arthur were out of immediate danger – although the child's head and bedclothes were saturated with blood, the wound was of a superficial nature – he went to No. 23 to check on his mother. He found Ann in a serious condition, and sent for Dr Wimberley.[216]

Dr Wimberley, who fortuitously also lived on Much Park Street, arrived at James Elkington's house just before ten and examined Harriett. He found the entrance wound of a bullet on the point of her right shoulder and a small abrasion on the pit of the stomach, which had been caused by the pressure of the steel busk in her corset – the metal stopping the bullet, and saving her life. The following morning Wimberley returned and extracted the bullet, buried three inches below the entry wound.[217]

Later that night James's eighteen year old son Richard[218] discovered a bullet under the chair on which Harriett had been sitting. It was split from having struck the steel busk.[219]

215 *Coventry Times*, 2nd June 1880.

216 Testimony of James Elkington. *Coleshill Chronicle*, 10th July 1880. Conrad Christopher Wimberley was born in Lincolnshire in 1839, but spent his formative years in London. He married Elizabeth Ann Morecraft at St John the Evangelist in north London in February 1863, the couple going on to have three children. Wimberley was educated at Edinburgh and St Andrews Universities, becoming MD at the latter in 1862. He practiced at the Middlesex Hospital later in 1862 before relocating to Coventry, where he was practising by 1864. In November 1871 he was voted a medical officer on the Board of the Coventry and Warwickshire Hospital, a post he held until 1883. His address in the 1870s and early 1880s was 21 Much Park Street – a much grander residence than the houses nearby in which Ann Elkington, James Twigger and others lived, boasting four bedrooms, separate dining and breakfast rooms, a wine cellar and stables. His last appearance in the Coventry newspapers came in January 1890. He died on 21st January 1906 in Wales aged 66.

217 Testimony of Dr Conrad Wimberley. *Coventry Times*, 7th July 1880.

218 A watchmaker's apprentice, Richard married Ada Carter in May 1886 and the couple had two children before his death in 1897, aged just thirty five.

219 Testimony of Richard Elkington. *Coleshill Chronicle*, 10th July 1880.

The doctor next went to examine Ann Elkington at her house along Much Park Street, and found her sitting in a chair. On examining her upper arm he noted that no bullet was embedded in her flesh – it had passed right through.[220] The wound to her stomach was far less serious than first feared.

At the Half Moon, Dr Fenton[221] arrived and examined Maria Feltham in her bedroom. He found a small wound in the back of her left hip, and the clothes cut where the bullet had passed through. A further examination the following day revealed a hard substance, undoubtedly the bullet, lodged six inches into the flesh below the entry wound. The victim declined having it removed.[222]

Henry Jennings was taken to the Coventry and Warwickshire Hospital; James Pallett walked the few yards to his home.

Oliver Style, now sitting calmly in a police cell, was remanded to appear before the magistrates.

*

The shocking rampage immediately made the pages of national newspapers, with one commenting – with tongue firmly in cheek, but which could be from the press of today – how very un-English the notion of a gunman running amok in the streets seemed:

"HE WENT IN FOR A SHOOT.

> Oliver Style, of Coventry, if not an American, is cursed with some of our lively cousins' least desirable peculiarities. It seems that he not only carries a revolver, but that he amuses himself in his leisure by shooting at targets. On a recent occasion Oliver,

220 Testimony of Dr Conrad Wimberley. *Atherstone, Nuneaton and Warwickshire Times*, 17th July 1880.

221 Dr Mark Fenton was educated at Trinity College, Dublin, and took his BA in 1869. He became a Doctor of Medicine in 1873. He began treating the population of Coventry in 1870 when he was appointed House Surgeon at the Coventry and Warwickshire Hospital, and was appointed Medical Officer of Health by Coventry City Council in 1874. He married Martha Marriott, daughter of Alderman James Marriott, in September 1874. Fenton died on 6th April 1897 aged just forty-eight. For a full obituary see the *Midland Daily Telegraph*, 7th April 1897.

222 *Atherstone, Nuneaton and Warwickshire Times*, 17th July 1880.

like his trans-Atlantic prototype, had been drinking to such an extent that he mistook human beings for targets to which he was accustomed,[223] and he blazed away with such success that he lodged bullets in the bodies of no less than six different people. Happily the law of England resents the taking of such liberties with the bodies of other people, and consequently Mr Style finds himself reduced to the inconvenience of making calculations as to the exactitude with which he could hit the nails with which the door of his cell is studded – a calculation which is not by any means profitable, for it is not likely that he will be able to amuse himself with his favourite playthings at any rate for a very considerable period. Commencing in the Half Moon Inn, his first shot broke a man's leg, with a second he lodged a bullet in a man's hand, and then taking a running shot he struck the landlady in the back. He then went to the house where his wife was staying, and with the other three shots he wounded his wife, child and mother-in-law respectively. Of course Style, though by each fresh essay manifesting surprising evidence of his skill with the revolver, could not be allowed to find human targets indiscriminately and for an indefinite period of time, and ultimately he was persuaded to desist operations by a policeman, and left to cogitate in a police cell on the success he had already achieved. What a text is the above incident from which to expatiate upon the criminal folly of habitually carrying firearms! Thank heaven the habit is un-English, and may it ever remain so."[224]

223 There is no suggestion that Oliver Style had been drinking, beyond the small glass of ale served by Maria Feltham's mother immediately before the shooting began.

224 *Portsmouth Evening News*, 1st June 1880.

5.

THE TRIAL

"THE ATTEMPTED MURDERS AT COVENTRY.

THE PRISONER BEFORE THE MAGISTRATES

On Thursday morning,[225] at the Coventry City Police Court, before the Mayor, H. Scampton, Esq,[226] and J. Marriott, Esq,[227] Oliver Style, Far Gosford Street, watchmaker, was charged with having feloniously shot his wife, Harriett Style, with intent to commit murder, on the 27th May last.

Long before eleven o'clock the precincts of the Court were thronged with people, and the liveliest interest was manifested in the case. When the doors were opened, all the available seats were quickly appropriated, but arrangements were made to prevent overcrowding. The prisoner, who walked into Court in a dejected manner, appeared to be weak and ill, and a chair was placed in the dock for his use. While the witnesses were giving evidence he appeared to take but little interest in the

225 1st July 1880.

226 Grocer and wine dealer Henry Scampton (1821-1890) represented Coventry's Spon Street Ward between 1865-1877, when he was elevated to Alderman of the City. He was appointed Mayor of Coventry in November 1878, and re-elected the following year. The position was filled by Henry Matterson in November 1880. Scampton's daughter Mary became a prominent campaigner for women's rights. [*Coventry Standard*, 16th November 1877; *Coventry Herald*, 15th November 1878.]

227 James Marriott was a well-known surveyor and builder, and was responsible for the planning and construction of Chapel Fields for the watchmaking community. A pillar of Coventry society, he had long served as Alderman and was appointed Mayor in both 1865 and 1866.

> proceedings, but in his examination of his wife and others he showed that he was far from being inattentive to what was going on. Mrs Style, who appeared with her right arm in a sling, and Mrs Elkington, were accommodated with seats.
>
> Mr Minster appeared to prosecute on behalf of the police, and said that he would content himself simply with calling witnesses, and not take up the time of the Court by making any observations. He would not be able to complete the case that day, but intended at a later hour to apply for an adjournment.
>
> The prisoner was undefended."[228]

The fact that Oliver Style decided against appointing a lawyer, and represented himself, could be seen as confirmation that he had a high opinion of himself – as indicated by his adding 'Cromwell' to his name. His only line of defence at the magistrates' hearing was attempting to prove that he'd been pushed into committing the horrendous acts by his wife's refusal to return home.

The sole witness he called was his eldest son, Oliver Jr, who had been to Much Park Street on several occasions to ask his mother to come home. The boy commented that he knew his father worked hard to support the family.[229]

Harriett readily agreed, telling the boy's father: "I have had eight children, and you have always been a good father to them, but a bad husband to me."[230]

But she refused to entertain the suggestion that she had provoked her husband's actions, telling the Bench:

> "There was no reason whatever that he should be jealous of either White or Goddard. There has been no improper intimacy between myself and either of these men, and nothing but what a husband might know. That I swear."[231]

Style's line of defence was over.

228 *Coventry Times*, 7th July 1880.
229 *Atherstone, Nuneaton and Warwickshire Times*, 17th July 1880.
230 *Coventry Times*, 7th July 1880.
231 *Coleshill Chronicle*, 10th July 1880.

By contrast, prosecuting counsel Oliver Minster[232] called a parade of witnesses, each of whom added to what was already a bleak picture against the defendant.

Style sat in the dock, resting his head on his arm and staring at the floor. Once or twice his lifted his head to look at a new witness as they took the stand, but he asked no questions, simply shaking his head when given the opportunity. When he heard the claim that he had intended to kill his son, Arthur, he became visibly upset and shook his head violently.[233]

At the beginning of the proceedings neither Ann Elkington and Henry Jennings had been able to attend the Magistrates' Court to give evidence due to their injuries.

Mrs Elkington's health had deteriorated since being first examined by Dr Wimberley, and the medical man told the court that she was now suffering from 'nervous depression' as a result of the severe wound to her arm. Consequently, it was decided by the magistrates to visit her at her home to hear her evidence. This meant the prisoner attending as well; when Oliver Style was informed of this, and told to prepare for a journey from Warwick Gaol back to Coventry, he was apparently greatly agitated at the thought of returning to the scene of his actions.

As they pulled up at Much Park Street few locals were aware of what was happening. But when he was taken out of the cab word soon spread, and an excited crowd soon grew outside the house.[234]

232 Oliver Minster was the last member of the well-known family of Coventry lawyers, founded by his grandfather Thomas Minster in 1793. He was born in January 1843, and having been admitted a solicitor in 1857 at the tender age of fourteen learned his craft in London. He returned to Coventry to take over the running of the practice on the death of his father Robert in 1873. The company still had the same offices in Trinity Churchyard as when founded eighty years earlier. Oliver Minster served fifteen years on the Town Council, and was solicitor to a great many city companies, including the Coventry Watchmakers' Friendly and Provident Society, and was a founder member of the Coventry Fire Brigade, at the time a volunteer-only force. He died in April 1906 aged seventy-three, having acted as a lawyer for almost fifty years.

233 *Coventry Herald*, 4th June 1880.

234 *Cheltenham Mercury*, 5th June 1880.

The Coventry and Warwickshire Hospital,
where Henry Jenning's deposition was taken.

Henry Jennings was also in a perilous state. By the end of June his condition had greatly worsened as inflammation set in to the wound, and Dr Wimberley had decided the only way to save the man's life was to amputate the limb. But on 29th June it seemed that such an operation would probably be fatal, such was Jennings' frailty, and it was decided to take his deposition from his bedside at the Hospital that evening. Jennings detailed how Oliver Style had marched into the tap room and shot him in the thigh, just about the knee. He said he had been in Style's company before, and never known him to act so violently. After half an hour the exhausted Jennings was left in peace, and Style was escorted back to Warwick Gaol by Chief Warder Cook and another officer. The leg was amputated the following day.[235]

Jennings was still lying in his hospital bed when Oliver Style was committed for trial by the magistrates on 23rd July, charged with

235 *Coventry Times*, 30th June 1880.

> "Having, on the 27th day of May, 1880, at the Parish of St Michael, in the City of Coventry, feloniously wounded his wife, Harriett Style, by shooting at her with a loaded revolver, with intent to murder."[236]

Identical charges were made out in respect of Ann Elkington and Maria Feltham.

There was much for Oliver Style to contemplate over the next twelve days while in the Warwick cells awaiting his turn in the dock.

*

'THE ATTEMPTED MURDERS IN COVENTRY.

TRIAL OF THE PRISONER – THE SENTENCE.

> At the Crown Court, Warwickshire Assizes, on Wednesday,[237] before Mr Justice Field,[238] Oliver Style (37), watch finisher, Coventry, was indicted for having on the 27th last, feloniously shot at and wounded Harriett Style, his wife, Ann Elkington, and Maria Feltham, with intent to murder them.
>
> The prosecution was conducted by Mr Ewins-Bennett (instructed by Mr O. Minster, Coventry); and at the request of the Judge, on Tuesday, Mr Stangye undertook the prisoner's defence.
>
> The circumstances of the case are already well known. It was alleged on the part of the prosecution that on the 27th May last prisoner went to the Half Moon Inn, Coventry, where he

236 Assizes: Midland Circuit: Indictment Files (National Archives: ASSI 12/13).

237 4th August 1880.

238 William Ventris Field (1813-1907) was called to the Bar in 1850 at the Inner Temple, after having practised for some time as a special pleader. He joined the Western circuit, but soon exchanged it for the Midland. He became a QC in 1864, and in 1875 was raised to the Bench as a Justice of the Queen's Bench. Justice Field was considered an excellent judge, fair and content to stay in the background. He retired from the Bench in 1890, becoming Baron Field of Bakeham, Surrey, spending much of his time in the House of Lords in the hearing of appeals. Lord Field died in 1907 aged 95.

deliberately shot Maria Feltham, in the back, with a revolver; also seriously wounding two other men at the same time and place. He then proceeded to the residence of his wife (then living apart from him) and fired at her, losing a bullet in her body, and also shooting at and wounding his mother-in-law, Mrs Elkington, in the arm. When taken into custody he stated that he had done what he had intended to do, and they could take him.

On Monday morning last it transpired that Mrs Elkington was too ill to attend, and Mr Ewins-Bennett applied for her depositions to be sent up to the Grand Jury, and having produced that necessary legal authority, the order was made. The Grand Jury found a true bill against the prisoner on Monday, and on Tuesday the Judge requested Mr Stangye to undertake the defence.

The evidence of Mrs Style having been taken, Mr Stangye cross-examined her, but without shaking her testimony in the slightest. She denied that any of the quarrels were caused by jealousy on the part of the prisoner.

Mrs Elkington also gave her evidence, and was not cross-examined.

James Twigger, labourer, also spoke as to seeing prisoner fire twice at his wife, and Edward Davis corroborated him. Whilst this witness was giving his evidence, the prisoner exclaimed, "You villain; I hope the Lord will strike you dead, you villain."

Thomas Upton, carpenter, Far Gosford Street, deposed to picking up prisoner's revolver which he had thrown into the air. PS Gray produced the revolver and PC Sale produced the box of cartridges.

Mr C.C. Wimberley, surgeon, produced the bullet, and stated the result of his examinations as already given.

William J. Veasey gave evidence as to the occurrences at the Half Moon Inn, after which Mr Ewins-Bennett briefly summed up. He warned the jury that the defence might wish to lessen the intent, and say that because he shot at so many he might shoot anyone, but he must draw their attention to the deliberate acts of the prisoner. If they thought the circumstances of the case warranted them in finding the prisoner guilty on the second count of the indictment – the intent to do grievous bodily harm – they might do so, but he did not suppose for a moment that they would. The intention of a man could only be arrived at by the acts which he commits. He did not think they could relieve their consciences by finding him guilty of the second count after the evidence they had heard.

Mr Stangye, for the defence, said that the jury could give four verdicts: 1st, that of Guilty of wounding with intent to murder; 2nd, that of Wounding with intent to do grievous bodily harm; 3rd, that of Unlawful wounding, and 4th, that the prisoner was Not Guilty. He could not ask them to acquit the prisoner altogether, and the utmost he could look forward to was that he would be found Guilty of unlawfully wounding. The facts proved that the wounds were inflicted by the prisoner by unlawful means, and it was therefore impossible to have any defence to a charge of the description referred to as the third. If they were satisfied beyond all reasonable doubt that he was guilty of the first count, and that it was his intention to take the life of his wife, they would have to say so. But if they thought there was any doubt of the intent, they would find him guilty of one of the minor charges. They might think that the prisoner's conduct was that of a maniac, or one of that condition, but it was not in his power to suggest that, as there was no evidence of it, but they must take the facts of the prisoner's frenzied state into their consideration. He did not wish to screen the prisoner from his proper punishment, but he suggested that it was not proved, beyond doubt, that the intent to murder existed.

The Judge then commenced his summing up, and characterised the charge as one of a very serious character, second only in gravity to wilful murder. He then explained the counts in the indictment, and said that he had more confidence in the jury than to think they would be seduced by such a blind, miserable offer as had been made by the counsel of the defence. They must not hesitate to do their duty, although it might be a painful one. The offence had not been committed in the heat and frenzy of the moment, but it was all done in the most deliberate manner. He went and bought deliberately a deadly weapon, which was made for nothing but to kill, and fired at a vital part of the woman. Sometimes deadly weapons were fired to frighten people, as in the case of poachers, but they had heard evidence that it was not fired for that purpose. The prisoner bought a deadly weapon, capable of producing death. If they found a man buying a deadly weapon and directing it at the heart of a woman, within a foot of her body, what could they think was his intention except to commit murder. The man was not drunk, and no attempt was made to say that he was; whilst at Birmingham his conduct,

> when he completed a regular commercial transaction in a most regular and business-like manner, was perfectly rational. The meaning of the language used by him, when he said, "Now I have got my revenge," left no doubt of what was his intention when he purchased the pistol. After a few other directions to the jury, they were ordered to consider their verdict.
>
> Without leaving the box, the Jury[239] intimated that they were agreed upon their verdict, which was that the prisoner was Guilty on the first count, viz. that of wounding with intent to murder.'[240]

The prosecution then confirmed that they did not intend to continue with the charges concerning Ann Elkington and Maria Feltham, and matters were then adjourned until the following morning.[241]

On Thursday, 5th August Oliver Style was brought up for sentencing. Bursting into tears, he told the court that he had a few things to say.[242]

> "In answer to the usual question whether he had any reason to show why sentence should not be passed upon him he said all his troubles had arisen out of the charge of assault made against him before the magistrates, of which he was innocent.[243] After that his wife had left him, and refused to return although he

239 James Rowe (a fifty-four year old lodging keeper of Leamington); Robert Herring (a thirty-two year old draper of Stratford-upon-Avon); Benjamin Crosby (a forty-one year old screw-ring and cabinet brass manufacturer of Birmingham); William Thomas French (a forty-two year old garden syringe maker); Thomas Gascoyne (a forty-two year old coachman from Stratford- upon-Avon); William Hunt (a fifty-seven year old engine fitter from Birmingham); Joseph Smallwood (a sixty-eight year old draughtsman from Aston); John Elliott (a forty-nine year old mason from Rugby); Joseph Cotley Cheshire (a thirty-four year old coach painter from Coleshill); William Ketch (a forty-nine year old optician from Birmingham); Thomas Priest (a seventy-one year old builder from Meriden); and William Kirkland (a thirty-five year old commercial traveller from Aston). List of jurors' names from 'Assizes: Midland Circuit: Crown Minute Books: 1873 Winter-1882 Winter' (National Archives: ASSI 11/33). Ages and occupations from 1881 census.

240 *Leamington Spa Courier*, 7th August 1880.

241 Ibid.

242 *Liverpool Mercury*, 6th August 1880.

243 The summons by William Henry White for assault.

repeatedly sent messages asking her to do so. Her refusal made him mad, and drove him out of his mind. He knew he had done a bad and rascally act, and he was sorry. He also asked why his witness had not been called.[244]

Lord Justice Field.

His Lordship in passing sentence told the prisoner that his counsel had exercised a proper discretion in not calling his witness, as if called it would have increased the gravity of the offence. Counsel's duty was to exercise his own judgement with reference to the interests committed to his care, and if a client insisted on the adoption of a course which he considered inconsistent with the interests and justice of the case, it was his duty to revoke the authority given him, rather than yield to a client's imprudent and improper urgency. He would give the prisoner credit for believing in a state of things which led him to believe that he had wrongs to avenge. This was not permitted by morality or religion, and the law condemned it in the strongest possible language. He dreaded to think of the sentence which he would have had to pass if the bullet which prisoner aimed at his wife's heart had proved fatal. Providentially for the prisoner and his wife, the course of the bullet was diverted by the woman's stays. His mother-in-law and other persons were the subjects of this vindictive attack. It had been suggested by Counsel that the prisoner was in a state of mind in which he was not responsible for his actions. There was a great popular error on that subject. It was suggested that a lighter punishment should be inflicted if a man could control his revengeful feelings and indulged them as the prisoner had done. It would be impossible to administer criminal justice if what was called uncontrollable impulse was to be admitted as a reason why a crime should not be punished. He

244 Presumably son Oliver Thomas Style, but possibly Henry White himself.

> had taken into account the prisoner's previous good character, but he could not pass over with a light sentence such a deliberate attempt on human life."[245]

Mr Justice Field then sentenced the prisoner to twenty-five years' penal servitude. Had it not been for the supposed previous good conduct, he would have awarded life imprisonment.[246]

In what was reported as a 'fainting condition',[247] Oliver Style was taken down by warders and returned to his cell to begin his sentence.

*

After three weeks of preparation by the prison authorities, on 26th August Oliver was loaded into a closed prison van along with four other prisoners and transported a hundred miles to north London and his new home, Pentonville Prison, where he was registered as Prisoner G759.[248]

Pentonville Prison.

245 *Coventry Times*, 7th August 1880.
246 *Glasgow Evening Post*, 6th August 1880.
247 *Coventry Times*, 11th August 1880.
248 Prison Commission Records, 1770-1951. Pentonville Prison: Register of Prisoners.

Three weeks later, having been fitted for his grey prison uniform – with black arrows pointing upwards – and his head shorn, it was time for Oliver Style to have his new prisoner photograph taken. On 16th September he was shepherded into a room alongside fourteen fellow new inmates – men such as William Albert, a comedian sentenced to six years for larceny; John Evans, a grocer sentenced to ten years for arson; and Herbert Plumley, a policeman sentenced to ten years for manslaughter.[249] Each awaited their turn in front of the camera's gaze, and as dictated by prison rules each raised their hands to their chest, so that any tattoos or other distinguishing marks could be recorded. In Oliver's case, it clearly showed that the tip of his left forefinger was missing.

A warder signed each photograph to certify its true likeness to the prisoner, and it was then inserted into the Pentonville album.[250]

With the reduction in transportation to destinations such as Australia, and crimes with the death penalty as a possible sentence reduced, Pentonville had been opened in 1842 with the intention of housing prisoners who had been sentenced to long-term imprisonment. It could hold 520 inmates, each of whom had their own cell measuring thirteen feet long, seven feet wide and nine feet tall.

Prisoners were forbidden to speak to one another, and would wear brown masks made of cloth to prevent them from seeing their neighbour when out on exercise. Their daily visits to chapel saw them sit in individual cubicles, their heads hidden from each other but visible to the warders.

Each prisoner was made to work from six in the morning until

249 Prison Commission Records, 1770-1951. Pentonville Prison: Register of Prisoners. Thirty-two year old Herbert Plumley had served as a constable in the Glamorganshire County force for ten years, when on the night of 21st April 1880 he punched a colliery watchman named Thomas Fowley in the face after the latter had struck him from behind with a length of wood. Fowley fell to the ground, striking his head, and never regained consciousness. See *South Wales Daily News*, 28th April 1880.

250 Prison Commission Records, 1770-1951: Pentonville Prison. A decade later, prison officers placed an angled mirror behind each new inmate so that the camera would capture both front and side profile in one shot.

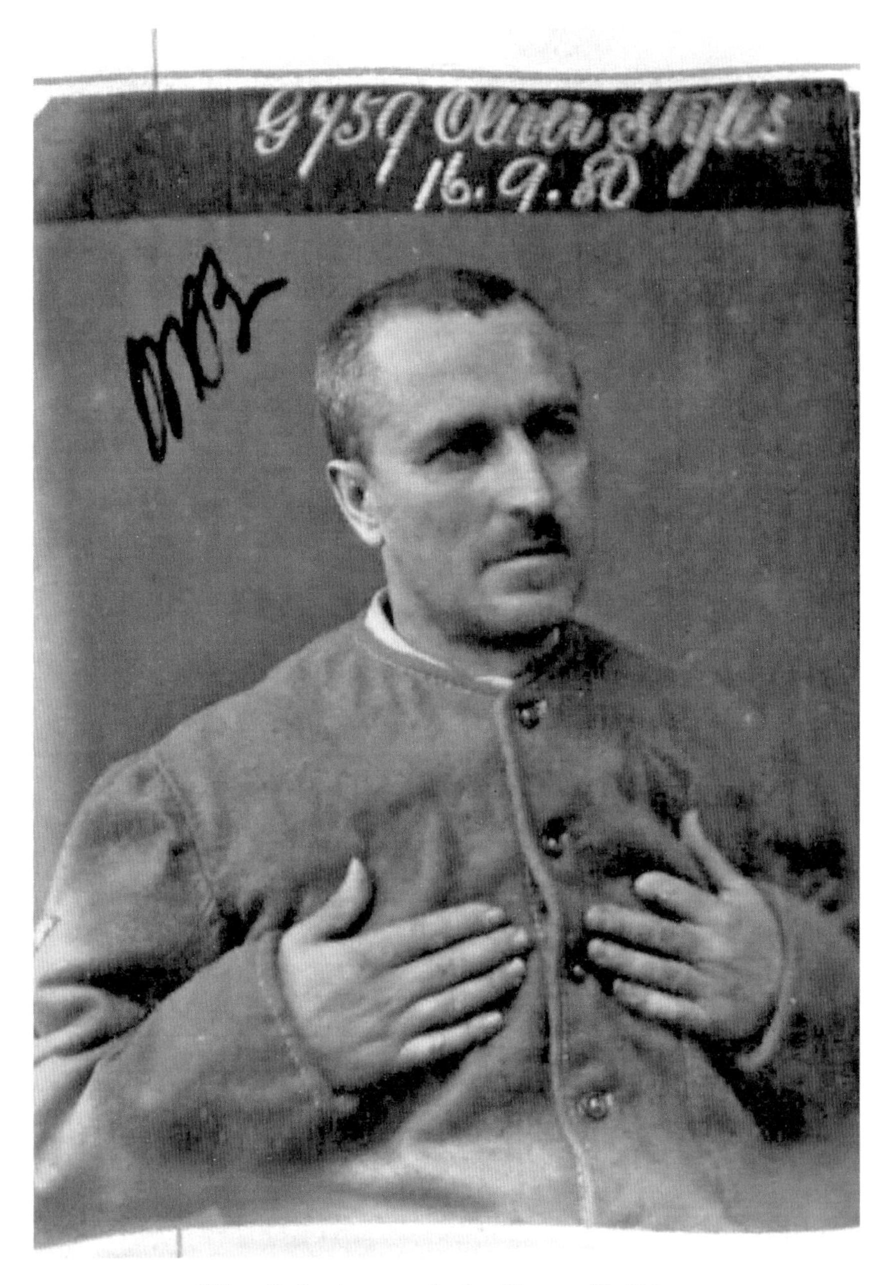

Oliver Style photographed at Pentonville Prison
on 16th September 1880.

seven at night, and tasks included picking oakum and weaving.[251] Oliver Style was immediately put to work at single-hand loom-weaving. He later said that, despite it being alien at first, he soon mastered the skill.[252]

251 See www.capitalpunishment.uk.org/penton.html. For a sense of a convict's life inside Pentonville, see Lewis Owens's excellent *The Pentonville Experiment: Prison. Addiction. Hope.* (2018).

252 Interview with Oliver Style following his release, as reported in the *Coventry Herald and Free Press*, 21st December 1900.

6.

AFTERMATH

As he began adjusting to his new life, having left Coventry for at least the next two decades, those who had been affected by Oliver Style's rampage at the Old Half Moon were attempting to return to their normality.

Some found it easier than others. Just five months after the shooting James Styles,[253] who had welcomed his friend Oliver into the tavern on that fateful evening, was summoned to appear before magistrates for refusing the leave the same pub at closing time when asked to do so by Maria Feltham. Prosecutor Mr Minster was back in court, this time informing the magistrates that Mrs Feltham "wished to keep the house respectable, if possible" – a tall order, given its recent history. James Styles sheepishly pleaded Guilty, and was fined 6s expenses.[254]

Maria Feltham herself continued as landlady of the Old Half Moon for almost a year, and is recorded on the 1881 census there with her children, now fourteen and eleven, and her mother Sarah Francis.[255]

However, just a month after the enumerator had completed his

253 James Styles continued to live at 19 Hertford Place for some years. By the time of the 1891 census he had relocated to his native London, taking wife Mary Ann with him, and worked as a builder while living at Great Marlborough Street. He returned to Coventry at some point before the 1901 census, following the death of his wife.

254 *Kenilworth Advertiser*, 23rd October 1880.

255 1881 census.

rounds Maria married Londoner Humphrey Welch, a thirty-one year old watch finisher[256] whose wife and only child had died seven years earlier,[257] and left the tavern.[258]

The couple moved back to their native London, where they lived for many years in Croydon, to the south of the capital,[259] and then in Highbury to the north, where Humphrey died in February 1919.[260]

Maria followed him on 1st September 1922, still living on the same street. She was seventy-five years old.[261] The bullet in her hip was never removed, and she no doubt felt a reminder of her tangle with Oliver Style every day for the last forty-two years of her life.

James Pallett, shot through the thumb as he attempted to protect

256 Marriage certificate of Humphrey Welch and Maria Feltham, 16th May 1881.

257 Humphrey Welch married Emma Farmer at Coventry in September 1873, and a son – Humphrey Jr – was born the following year. Tragically, both mother and son died during the birth.

258 It's not clear who took over the running of the Old Half Moon following Maria Feltham's departure. In *Kelly's Directory of Warwickshire* for 1886 the landlord was recorded as Charles Stafford, who transferred the licence to Frederick William Asbury in 1889 (*Coventry Herald*, 2nd August 1889). The Asbury family ran the pub until 1903 (trade directories), when it was taken over by William Judd. An article in the *Coventry Evening Telegraph* of 19th August 1955 reporting on Mr Judd's death stated that he ran the Old Half Moon until it was closed in 1930. At that point the licence was surrendered in favour of an off licence called the Godiva Stores on Three Spires Avenue. 27 Hertford Place was soon converted to a private residence. The *Coventry Evening Telegraph* of 29th October 1932 reported a strange occurrence when Bernard Walker, living at the address, heard a moan outside his door and on investigating found a man lying in the street in great pain. The man, who proved to be William Latham of 17 Hertford Square, died in hospital. Hertford Square was demolished to make way for the construction for the Ring Road, and most of the buildings in Hertford Place went at the same time, although the road remains.

259 1891 and 1901 census returns.

260 Probate record of Humphrey Welch, leaving £2,811 2s 4d to his widow Maria.

261 Death certificate of Maria Welch, showing the cause as 'fatty' infiltration of the heart, and gastric catarrh. Her estate of £2,865 14s was left to her daughter Sarah Feltham, who had married John Flinn in March 1888 at Shoreditch, east London. The couple had two sons and a daughter. Sarah died in June 1939. Maria's son, Joseph Feltham Jr, relocated to Kent and married Maud Jeffreys there in October 1909. They had one daughter, Iris. Joseph died in January 1949.

himself, returned to his life as a watchmaker, although the wound no doubt hampered his work for some time. He and his wife Harriet remained at 5 Hertford Square[262] until James's death there on 13th October 1890, aged fifty-one.[263]

The worst affected of the Old Half Moon victims was Henry Jennings. Even before the shootings he had experienced tragedy, when his wife of twelve years, Harriet, died early in 1876.[264] Left with three young daughters ranging from seven to two, Henry continued his business as a baker while living at 15 Hertford Place, and in 1878 married Catherine Wallis.[265]

A month after the trial and conviction of Oliver Style the *Coventry Herald* published a letter from a correspondent who signed himself 'ANXIOUS'.[266] In it, the writer voiced concerns over the welfare of Henry Jennings and his young family, now that the baker had seen his injury result in the amputation of his leg:

> "Sir, – I have been thinking for some time past that I should see an appeal on behalf of the unfortunate victim of the Coventry shooting case, May 27th last, Henry Jennings. I hope the public will not lose sight of the necessity of procuring him a leg, as with that he would be able to earn a livelihood and maintain his family, but without it he is unable to do anything.
>
> It is truly grievous to see the poor fellow going about on his crutches, and no effort being made to assist him, when a little from a generous public would be that means of placing him in a position of comparative independence, by enabling him to follow his trade (a baker).
>
> Hoping some philanthropic person will take up his cause."[267]

262 1881 census.
263 Death certificate of James Pallett, which shows that he died after suffering a year with tuberculosis, resulting in him coughing up blood.
264 Civil Registration Death Index, 1837-1915: Harriet Jennings.
265 Marriage certificates of Henry Jennings and Harriet Ison (1864) and Henry Jennings and Catherine Wallis (1878); 1871 and 1881 census; *Kelly's Directory of Warwickshire*, 1876.
266 A later report names the writer as Mr W. Meddows, Honorary Secretary of the Coventry Master Bakers' Association (*Coventry Herald*, 8th October 1880).
267 'Letters to the Editor', *Coventry Herald*, 17th September 1880.

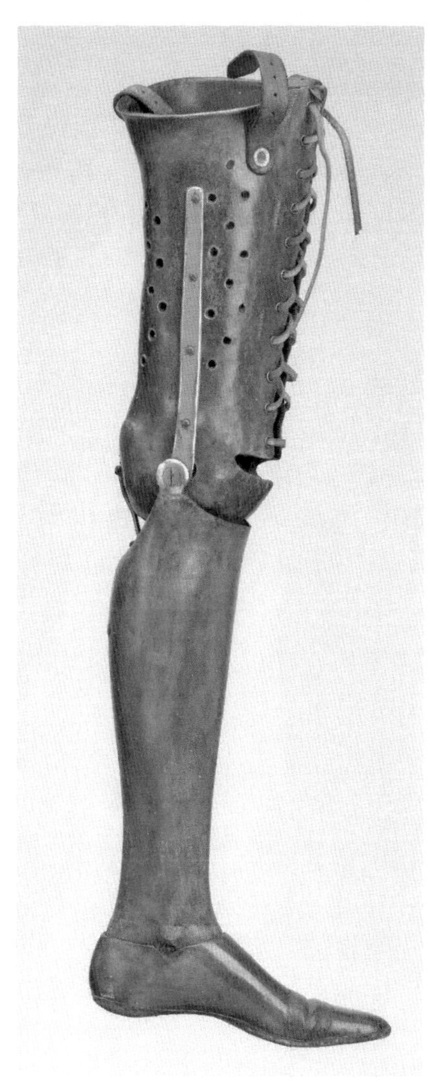

An artificial leg from
the late Nineteenth century.

'Anxious' needn't have worried. Within three weeks the same newspaper reported that a fund had been set up, and several donations already received, with the intention of paying for an artificial leg to be provided for Jennings.[268]

A month later, on 3rd November, it was reported that some £37 had been raised – £2,500 today – and this would be used to purchase flour and other items to allow Jennings to start in business. Two committee members went to Birmingham to see the leading artificial limb manufacturer,[269] Mr Salt of 21 Bull Street,[270] who informed them that he would be pleased to make a first-class leg for £15 15s, the trade price being £21. Henry would, said Mr Salt, "be able to use it with ease and comfort in a very short time by active perseverance and care on his

268 *Coventry Herald*, 8th October 1880.

269 *Coventry Times*, 3rd November 1800.

270 Salts was founded in the 1750s by brothers John and William Salt as a 'surgeon instrument maker'. They moved to their premises on Bull Street in 1845. The firm received a Royal Warrant in 1863, and in that decade began to concentrate on medical products. Their artificial limbs were in great demand thanks to the horrors of the Great War. Salts Healthcare is still trading today, as a leading international medical device manufacturer. They have an annual turnover of an estimated £25million.

own part."[271]

By the end of the month all was ready. A list of subscribers published in the *Coventry Times* of 24th November 1880 reported the heartwarming news that the great and the good of Coventry had donated a total of £65 11s,[272] and this had been used to provide Jennings with flour, coal and other items, and he was about to open a small shop as a baker and provisions dealer at 7 Thomas Street, off the Butts.

It was also reported that the artificial leg, made of cork, would be ready a few days later – a full six months since the innocent Henry Jennings had been cruelly struck down by Oliver Style.[273]

It was at the Thomas Street address that Henry and his family were recorded the following April for the 1881 census, and over the next decade his fortunes certainly improved. Between 1890 and 1893 he saw all three daughters married.[274]

Curiously, in both the 1891 and 1901 census returns Henry is recorded as a boot maker, living at 28 Hertford Place – next door to the Old Half Moon. Had his experience with his artificial limb sparked an interest in a different career?

Henry Jennings died on 30th June 1909 after a sudden syncope – collapsing due to a sudden drop in blood pressure.[275] Was this related to his amputation nearly thirty years earlier?

*

Seven months after arriving at Pentonville, and ten after the events of 27th May, Oliver Style was transferred to Chatham Prison, in

271 *Coventry Herald*, 5th November 1880.
272 £4,500 today.
273 *Coventry Times*, 24th November 1880.
274 Sarah Ann to Joseph Clarke in 1890, Alice to John Wilson in 1892, and Roseanne to Arthur Gough in 1893.
275 Death certificate of Henry Jennings, registered 1st July 1909. His occupation was recorded as 'Shoe repairer'. Sadly, his widow Catherine appears in the 1911 census as residing at the Coventry Union Workhouse, where she died the following year.

Henry Jennings' youngest daughter Alice,
with her husband John Wilson.
Courtesy Bryan Ball

Kent.[276] He appears in the 1881 census, taken just six days later, as being thirty-eight years old, and married. His occupation is given as 'Convict'.

Situated on St Mary's Island in the River Medway, which ran through the dockyards in the north of the county, Chatham Gaol was opened in 1856. Accommodating around 1,700 prisoners, over the following decade convict labour was used to build the sea wall which protects the docks.

In 1880 the prison was selected to house men such as Oliver Style who had no previous convictions – so-called 'Star Class' convicts. They were kept apart from repeat offenders in the hope that they would not pick up criminal knowledge, thereby reducing the chance of them re-offending.[277]

Oliver was put to hard labour on the docks, where he would sweat away for the next two years.[278]

276 On 28th March 1881. Interview with Oliver Style following his release, as reported in the *Coventry Herald and Free Press*, 21st December 1900.

277 www.institutionalhistory.com.

278 Interview with Oliver Style following his release, as reported in the *Coventry Herald and Free Press*, 21st December 1900.

7.

THE BATTLE OF HEARSALL COMMON

Reader, imagine yourself in the position of being a member of Oliver Style's family in the aftermath of his conviction.

Do you keep yourself to yourself, quietly going about your business while the furore dies down and life returns to normal?

Or, like Oliver's brother-in-law Samuel Arnold, do you agree to participate in a bare-knuckle prize fight, watched by more than a hundred people, which results in the death of your opponent and a court appearance charged with manslaughter?

Samuel Arnold had married Oliver's sister Caroline Style – seemingly now a 'good girl' after her earlier brushes with the law – at St Mark's on 12th June 1871,[279] and over the course of the next decade the couple had gone on to welcome daughters Emma[280] and Mary Ann,[281] and son Robert.[282]

But by the 1880s, things had turned sour.

It wasn't as if Samuel didn't have previous; even before he and Caroline married he'd appeared in court, first at just sixteen years of age, receiving three months' imprisonment on 23rd July 1866 for absconding in April from his apprenticeship to an ironfounder,[283]

279 *Coventry Standard*, 16th June 1871.
280 1875-1949.
281 1877-1946.
282 1879-1937.
283 *Coventry Standard*, 28th July 1866.

then fourteen days' imprisonment in August 1869 for being drunk and disorderly in Greyfriars Lane.[284]

Three months before his marriage to Caroline he received a month for assault, this time after being arrested by PC Green in Little Park Street. Samuel was drunk, and on walking past a couple standing in the doorway of their home he verbally abused the wife. When her husband complained, he was punched in the mouth.[285]

In July 1875 Samuel was in the Royal Sailor Inn on Well Street when he took the opportunity to steal a purse containing two pawn tickets, a half-crown and a sixpence from Mary Bird.[286] He received a month in prison.

Five years later, in April 1880, a much more serious offence was committed. Arnold was brought before Magistrates Scampton and Soden on a charge of violently assaulting his three year old daughter Mary Ann,[287] by beating her with a strap at their home on Cox Street. The Chief Superintendent of Police told the Bench there had been frequent complaints of Arnold's treatment of his daughter.

A few days earlier, at half-past seven on the evening of Tuesday 20th April, a neighbour named Ann Chetwyn[288] had been standing outside her front door when she heard Arnold, home alone with the children, striking the little girl with a strap, shouting "Take that, you b————." The incident was also heard by another neighbour, Lucy McCall, who told the Court she also heard a beating being inflicted on the Wednesday morning.

Inspector Wyatt arrived on Thursday afternoon armed with a warrant, and Samuel Arnold was arrested. He admitted taking a strap to Mary Ann, but said it was his right to correct his children when necessary, adding that his young daughter was "a very dirty child".

284 *Coventry Herald*, 13th August 1869.
285 *Coventry Standard*, 25th February 1870.
286 *Coventry Herald*, 23rd July 1875.
287 Incorrectly called just 'Ann' in the newspaper report.
288 Aged fifty-two in 1880, Ann Chetwyn lived with her husband Henry at 2 Court 6 Street, Cox Street. [1881 census].

Cox Street, where the Arnold family were living
at the time of Samuel's beating of daughter Mary Ann.

Mary Ann was brought into court to display her injuries, and the description by a reporter from the *Coventry Herald* is harrowing:

> "At the rising of the Court on the previous day, a person brought the child and exhibited its back and legs, which were one mass of weals and bruises, so that a finger could scarcely be laid between them; the child's cheek had also a red and black bruise, and, altogether, she presented a most sickening appearance."

The magistrates were reminded that Arnold had appeared in front of the Bench several times – the reporter from the *Kenilworth Advertiser* claimed thirteen times[289] – and had therefore made himself liable to a sentence of six months' with hard labour. But the magistrates were mindful that a long custodial sentence would deprive Caroline and the children of much-needed funds, so sentenced him to two months' with hard labour, with the hope that this case would act as a caution.[290]

It did not work. In December that year Samuel Arnold was jailed

289 *Kenilworth Advertiser*, 1st May 1880.
290 *Coventry Herald*, 23rd April 1880.

for twenty-eight days for failing to pay maintenance for Caroline and the children,[291] after their separation following the beating of Mary Ann,[292] and to make matters worse Caroline was heavily-pregnant again.[293]

His failure to support his family saw them enter the Coventry Union Workhouse, with Caroline almost full-term. She gave birth there to another daughter, Alice, on 19th January 1881. We shall hear much more of little Alice later in this story. Caroline and the children were still in the Workhouse when the census for that year was taken, on 3rd April. Samuel is recorded as living with his widowed mother Emma at Cook Street.[294]

But if 1881 had started with Samuel Arnold being freed from Warwick Gaol, the year would end with him back behind bars.

*

Coventry had long been known for prize fighting, with some of the bare-knuckled pugilists earning a degree of fame through their efforts – and often a memorable nickname.

One February 1829 Bill Hayfield – 'the Flash Barber' – beat Jack Hammerton – 'the Chicken Butcher' – over half an hour of brutality, with the 'Barber' emerging the victor. On the same evening, at the Royal Oak on Gosford Street, a number of sparring matches took place between men including 'Ginger' Berry, 'Bacon' Smith, 'Fatty' Adrian, 'the Cockney Dyer' and 'the Living Skeleton'.[295]

In December 1850 two men, Samuel Gibbs and William Onions,

291 Calendar of Prisoners, 1868-1929: 1881, Samuel Arnold.

292 Thankfully Mary Ann Arnold appears to have gone on to lead a normal life. She married George Nickols in 1901 and had two surviving children, although three more died in infancy [1911 census]. She died in 1946 aged sixty-nine.

293 Caroline gave birth to daughter Alice in January 1881, meaning she would have conceived in late April 1880, around the time of her husband's arrest.

294 1881 census.

295 See David McGrory's entertaining *Bloody British History: Coventry* (2013) and John Ashby's must-read *The Character of Coventry* (2001) for a detailed look at the characters involved in the Coventry prize-fighting circuit of the early 1800s.

met on Whitley Common to resolve a difference of opinion over a sovereign which had arisen over a game of cards they had been playing at the Coombe Abbey tavern on Craven Street, which was kept by Gibbs. They had not gone far into the bout before police officers arrived to break up the gathering, and both were bound over to keep the peace for six months in lieu of a £20 fine.[296]

These and other fighters might have puffed out their chests with pride at the events of 26th September 1881, which ended with Samuel Arnold in deep trouble, for as the *Coventry Herald* wrote at the beginning of their coverage:

> "One of those brutal prize fights for which Coventry was celebrated half a century ago, but which of late years have fortunately been of very rare occurrences, took place on Monday last in the suburbs of the city, and one of the combatants either in the course of the fight or immediately afterwards received injuries which terminated fatally on Tuesday evening. The details of the affair are somewhat shrouded in mystery, for of course only persons who really know what took place are the bystanders, and those who participated in the fight."[297]

The facts of the matter are as follows.

The affair was rooted in an earlier fight between Samuel Arnold and his opponent, forty-five year old weaver John Plant,[298] following a quarrel at a tavern sometime in early August. Despite being fourteen years older than Arnold, Plant was seemingly in better shape – Samuel was five feet five-and-a-half inches tall, with a 'broad build'[299] (his nickname was 'Podge')[300] – and had beaten him on that occasion, and for the next seven weeks a grudge had been simmering between the two, with Plant and his supporters calling Arnold a coward. As his defence council would later state at

296 *Coventry Herald*, 13th and 20th December 1850.

297 *Coventry Herald*, 30th September 1881.

298 In *Bloody British History: Coventry* (2013), author David McGrory gives John Plant the nickname 'Jacco', but I have been unable to find any reference to this moniker in contemporary reports.

299 Calendar of Prisoners, 1868-1929: 1881, Samuel Arnold.

300 'Trial of the Prisoners'. *Coventry Herald*, 18th November 1881.

the eventual trial, "Arnold thought it incumbent on his honour to fight again."[301]

Finally it was agreed that a rematch would take place, with the winner taking the money put up by both parties.

On the evening of Sunday, 25th September, John Plant was in the Woolpack on St John's Street,[302] near his home, with a friend named David Warner when Samuel Arnold came in. The two had a conversation about the proposed fight, and Plant said that there would be no money put down that night, "but the following morning it would be all right."

The next day Plant and Warner went to see another acquaintance, a stonemason named Walter Newman, about advancing some money for Plant's contribution to the purse. Newman said he would "find a pound," to which Plant replied, "That will do. If I had money myself, I would not ask anyone."[303]

Between midday and one o'clock Plant and Warner went to the Charterhouse, where they met Samuel Arnold and awaited further instructions. The two fighters were quite friendly to one another. After at hour, the order came at last to head towards Whitley Common – the scene of the famous 1836 prize fight between 'Gammon' Shilton and 'Whopper' Flint – and as the three men approached they saw a large group of people waiting for them.[304]

At the same time, Sergeant Thomas Moore of the Coventry County Constabulary was on duty at Pinley. He saw the crowd of men congregating on the Fields, and as he walked towards them they moved off into Folly Lane. His policeman's intuition told him something was afoot, so he followed to London Road and saw them assembling on Whitley Common, where they were joined

301 *Coventry Herald*, 18th November 1881.

302 The Woolpack was open in 1790, and was run between 1835 and 1851 by Bob Randle, one of Coventry's most famous prize fighters. It closed in 1929 but was not demolished until 1962 as part of the Ring Road construction works.

303 Testimony of David Warner, *Coventry Herald*, 11th November 1881.

304 Testimony of David Warner, *Ashby-de-la-Zouch Gazette*, 15th October 1881.

by another crowd approaching from the direction of the city. There were, by now, close to a hundred and fifty men gathered.[305]

John Plant took off his neck tie and began loosening his clothing, saying, "I mean having a go here."[306]

But Sergeant Moore approached again, and once more the crowd dispersed, this time to Green Lane. As the officer followed, a man named Henry Twycross went up to him and asked, "Look here, policeman, here's two mates want to bring off a fight. Will you allow them to do it?" Moore replied in the negative, despite Twycross claiming no stake was involved. Realising the officer would not be swayed, Twycross informed the crowd and they started to move off in all directions.[307]

John Plant went with David Warner to the Salutation Inn on London Road,[308] and over a drink said he wouldn't fight that day after all.

They then went to a beer house known as 'the Wrexham' on Dead Lane,[309] where Henry Lapworth found them and told them the fight was back on – they were to make their way to the Broomfield Tavern close to the Butts,[310] where they would receive further

305 Testimony of Thomas Moore, *Ashby-de-la-Zouch Gazette*, 15th October 1881.

306 Testimony of David Warner, *Ashby-de-la-Zouch Gazette*, 15th October 1881.

307 Testimony of Thomas Moore, *Ashby-de-la-Zouch Gazette*, 15th October 1881.

308 Opened before the 1750s, the Salutation Inn was demolished in 1962.

309 There is some confusion as to the actual name of this tavern. Dead Lane was in the area of Much Park and Little Park Streets.

310 The earliest appearance of the Broomfield Tavern, on Broomfield Place, appears to be in 1855, when it was kept by a man named Joseph Bindley. In April that year an inquest was held into the death of four year old Jane Bradshaw, who lived with her family on the street. When her father returned to the house some children told him that his daughter had fallen into 'the pit', a water-filled area along a footpath leading from Broomfield Place which is now covered by the car park serving Coventry Rugby Club's ground. Despite her lungs being drained of water, and the young girl being put into a warm bath to revive her, Jane Bradshaw died of drowning (*Coventry Herald*, 20th April 1855). Landlord Joseph Bindley transferred the licence to John Royle in 1859, who in turn passed it on to John Crockford in 1861. Two years later he hanged himself in an upstairs

The Broomfield Tavern.

instructions.

They arrived and saw Samuel Arnold with some of his supporters, sitting in the 'front place'. After twenty minutes, and all those involved now in place, they left the Broomfield at four o'clock[311] and walked up the path under the railway viaduct, making their way to Hearsall Common,[312] stopping at the far end. Some sixty to seventy people were there, eagerly awaiting proceedings to commence.

They didn't have long to wait. Plant and Arnold removed their shirts, stripping down to their trousers and boots, then shook hands. They then began to fight.[313]

bedroom by knotting his neck-tie around a bed post (*Coventry Herald*, 2nd April 1863).

311 Testimony of David Warner, *Ashby-de-la-Zouch Gazette*, 15th October 1881.

312 Testimony of William Oswin, *Ashby-de-la-Zouch Gazette*, 15th October 1881.

313 Testimony of David Warner, *Ashby-de-la-Zouch Gazette*, 15th October 1881.

Hearsall Common.

For three or four rounds it was an even contest, with neither man knocked down, although Samuel Arnold's eye was almost completely closed. Then, as Plant advanced on his man, his foot slipped, and as his head and upper body lurched forward Arnold met him with a fearsome uppercut.[314]

From then, Plant was put down a dozen times, each time being lifted back to his feet by his 'second', bricklayer's labourer William Lapworth.[315] Eventually, after three-quarters of an hour, John Plant could take no more. Although on his feet, he was unable to raise his arms and seemed unable to continue. William Lapworth, no doubt having a financial stake in the matter, encouraged him despite shouts for Plant to stay down, including from Samuel Arnold himself.

Finishing the job, Arnold struck his opponent on both the left

314 Testimony of Alfred Cross, *Ashby-de-la-Zouch Gazette*, 15th October 1881.

315 Testimony of David Warner, *Ashby-de-la-Zouch Gazette*, 15th October 1881.

and right side of his body, and two heavy strikes to the nose. As Plant lurched and began to fall he caught him with a haymaker to the lower ribs.[316]

At last the fight was over. John Plant, semi-conscious on the ground, was unable to stand upright for some twenty minutes without help, so two of his supporters, David Warner and William Oswin, picked him up. Warner retrieved Plant's shirt from under a hedge and dressed the beaten man with the help of others. The rest of the crowd had already dispersed without bothering to check on Plant.

Propping him up between them, Warner and Oswin practically carried Plant along the road towards the Coombe Abbey on Craven Street,[317] a distance of only a mile but which took three-quarters of an hour. As Plant shuffled along his head hung low on his chest, and he mumbled incoherently.

At last they arrived at the Coombe Abbey, and it was just getting dark. On entering the tavern they saw that Samuel Arnold and his supporters were already enjoying a drink.

Arnold stood up and offered Plant his chair, and gave him two cups of tea, which he drank. Despite having some bread and butter brought to him he was unable to eat anything, and for the forty-five minutes he was in the pub didn't say a single word. All the while, blood flowed freely from a cut on the bridge of his nose.

Warner called a cab and took Plant back to his home on St John's Street. On the journey he asked the injured man a question, but received no reply.[318]

Plant's mother was at the house when they arrived, a little after eight o'clock, and later told the inquest that

316 Testimony of Alfred Cross, *Ashby-de-la-Zouch Gazette*, 15th October 1881.

317 Opened in 1850 when Craven Street and the Chapel Fields district was developed, the Coombe Abbey finally pulled its last pint in 2014 after 164 years of serving thirsty customers.

318 Testimony of David Warner, *Ashby-de-la-Zouch Gazette*, 15th October 1881.

> "He was insensible. He never spoke from the time he came home up till his death… I was with him nearly the whole of the time. He never spoke, and seemed quite insensible."[319]

A woman named Maria Chettem had been living with Plant for more than twenty years as his wife,[320] although the two were not married. When he was brought back to their rooms and placed in bed she went downstairs to fetch some water to clean him up, only to hear a sudden noise from the room above. She hurried back to the bedroom to find that, while still unconscious, John had slipped off the bed, feet first.[321]

Dr Wimberley, who examined the victims of Oliver Style's rampage the previous year, was called to the house at around half-past nine that evening, and later told magistrates the condition of the beaten man when he arrived:

> "I found him in bed, perfectly unconscious, face and eyes much swollen and bruised, chest and sides much bruised, three ribs broken on the left side, blood oozing from his mouth and nose, left hand much swollen and contused. I saw him three or four times before his death, which occurred on the following night. He never regained consciousness."[322]

John Plant died the following evening, unconscious, in his own

319 Inquest testimony of Elizabeth Pritchard, *Coventry Herald*, 30th September 1881.

320 'The Fatal Prize Fight Near Coventry', *Ashby-de-la-Zouch Gazette*, 15th October 1881. Born Maria Bradley in 1828 at Shipston on Stour, Warwickshire, she married James Chittem in 1848. They had five children together before parting; there is no record of James's death, but he is named on the baptism record of youngest child Ann, born in October 1866 and baptised in January 1873 – although this in itself doesn't mean he was alive. In the 1871 census Maria is listed as living with John Plant, who is recorded as being unmarried, with Maria 'living with above person'. Ten years later – five months prior to the fight – both John and Maria are listed as 'married', although there appears to be no record of a wedding. In the 1891 census Maria gave the name Chettem, and described herself as a widow. Who of, is uncertain. She died in 1896.

321 *Coventry Herald*, 14th October 1881.

322 'The Fatal Prize Fight Near Coventry', *Ashby-de-la-Zouch Gazette*, 15th October 1881.

bed.

That morning Sergeant Moore had arrived at the City Police Station and was told that the fight had taken place the previous afternoon, despite his best efforts. Instructed by Superintendent Hannah to arrest those involved in the spectacle, at five o'clock in the morning Moore went with PC Charles Duncuff[323] to the Hope and Anchor Inn at 38 Sherbourne Street,[324] where they found Samuel Arnold in the kitchen. His left eye was by this time completely closed, and both hands dark with bruises.[325] He was taken into custody.

Later that day the inquest into Plant's death opened at the Coventry and Warwickshire Hospital before Coroner Dewes.

Little evidence was given, as Dewes wished to adjourn in order to allow a post mortem to be carried out, but Plant's mother Elizabeth Pritchard – remarried to another man, William Pritchard, in 1874 – said that her son was a weaver, not in the habit of fighting.[326] Given his earlier beating of Arnold, and subsequent plan to win the prize-fight purse, she obviously didn't know him as well as she thought she did.

Over the next few days another eight men involved in the bout to some degree, from fixing the venue to raising the prize money, were arrested. They were remanded to await an appearance before the magistrates.

In the meantime the funeral of John Plant took place, on Sunday, 2nd October. The cortege passed through the streets of Coventry to St Mark's, with hundreds of people lining the route. It was reported that several thousand people gathered at the church itself to pay their respects, in the process causing considerable damage as they

323 Forename from 1881 census, which records twenty-three year old Charles Duncliff as a Police constable living as a boarder on Lockhurst Lane.

324 The Hope and Anchor opened in the 1820s, and was run in 1881 by watchmaker James Thompson. It was destroyed by bomb damage in November 1940.

325 'The Prisoners Committed for Trial', *Ashby-de-la-Zouch Gazette*, 15th October 1881.

326 *Coventry Herald*, 30th September 1881.

trampled over the graves. The service was read by Rev Gordon Sedgwick, vicar of St Mark's, as Plant was laid to rest.[327]

Six days later, at the conclusion of the inquest Dr Wimberley read out his post mortem report, revealing the horrific injuries suffered by John Plant:

> "External surface of body: Face much contused, especially the forehead, eyes, left side, and lower part of the ear. A contused lacerated wound on the left side of the nose half an inch in length, and leading to the fractured nasal bones. A large contusion on the left side of the front of the chest, extending from the clavicle to the third rib. Another large contusion on the left side, below the nipple, over the fifth and sixth ribs. A large contusion on the right side, above and external to the nipple. Several smaller contusions about the front of the chest, and anterior surface of both shoulders. Both hands contused, more especially the left, which was much swollen. No fracture of the bones of the hand.
>
> Head: Left temporal muscle much contused. On removing the skull cap a large quantity of coagulated blood (about three ounces) found effused over the whole of the right hemisphere of the brain beneath the *dura mater*. Veins of the surface of the whole brain much congested. Commencing inflammation of the membranes. Brain substance for a space of about two inches on the posterior and under surface of the right hemisphere contused, soft, and easily breaking down under the finger.
>
> Nasal bones fractured transversely and longitudinally, and comminuted, one fragment half of an inch square lying loose on the left side. Tissues over nasal bones much contused.
>
> Chest: Fourth, fifth and sixth ribs fractured, an inch external to the cartilages. Pleura not injured. Tissues external to the fractured ribs much contused."

Coroner Dewes voiced the thoughts of many during his summing up, when he commented:

> It seems disgraceful to me that such a thing should have happened close to a town like Coventry. You can hardly call it a fair fight, because the deceased man was forty-five years old, and the other

327 'Funeral of the Victim of the Fight', *Coventry Herald*, 7th October 1881.

> man only thirty-one. There was too great a disparity between the ages of the two men, for although no doubt Plant took care of himself up to a certain point, he could not be expected to last so well as the younger man."

In the face of such evidence, the jury wasted no time in returning a verdict of manslaughter against Samuel Arnold.[328]

The magistrates had concluded the same at their own hearing, and at the end of proceedings Arnold and his fellow prisoners were committed for trial at the Warwickshire Assizes. One reporter in court captured the mood of the public:

> "The prisoners were removed on Friday evening to Warwick Gaol. They were conveyed from the County Hall, where a large crowd had gathered, to the station in an omnibus from the Craven Arms [Hotel]. Great indignation was manifested by the crowd against the prisoners. Along the whole of the route that were groaned and hooted at, and in the Warwick Road several stones were thrown at and struck the omnibus.
>
> At the railway station a very large crowd had assembled, and the porters had the greatest difficultly in keeping the platform and premises clear. On the arrival of the omnibuses the prisoners were greeted with cries of "Drown them," "Hang them," "Crucify them," and groans and hisses.
>
> They were with difficulty got to the platform, from which they left by the 6.37pm train for Milverton, in charge of Sergeant Moore, and Constables Duncuff, Huddlestone and Borton."[329]

The nine men were brought up before Mr Justice Mathew on Thursday, 17th November 1881, and the jury had no hesitation in finding them all Guilty.

His Lordship Mr Justice Mathew, passing sentence, commented on the nature of the incident and where he saw the blame lying:

> "I am going to pass a lenient sentence – as I consider – but I

328 'The Inquest', *Ashby-de-la-Zouch Gazette*, 15th October 1881.
329 'The Prisoners Committed for Trial', *Ashby-de-la-Zouch Gazette*, 15th October 1881.

> hope it will be sufficient to warn people in the neighbourhood of their conduct in countenancing exhibitions of this character, and the serious consequences that may ensue to them if either men engaged in the fight meets with his death.
>
> I am willing to think of you prisoners, whom the jury had found to be bystanders, that you did not contemplate that any such terrible consequences would result to the poor man Plant as did ensue. I think, however, you ought to have interfered – that before the last three rounds began you ought to have stopped the fight – and that your criminality is that you did not do so."[330]

He sentenced Samuel Arnold to six months' imprisonment with hard labour; Walter Newman three months, William Lapworth and William Wright two each, and John Griffiths, William Cook, Henry Twycross, William Crump and Harry Lester both to one month imprisonment.[331] They were taken down.

Home Secretary Sir William Harcourt, concerned about the "recent epidemic of prize fighters", issued circulars to the Chairmen of Quarter Sessions across the country instructing them to pay special attention to such cases of 'breach of the peace'.[332]

*

On his release, on 13th May 1882, Samuel headed to Castle Street, Hillfields, and an improbable reconciliation with Caroline.[333] Their daughter Rose was born ten months later.[334] Another son, Walter, was born in 1885.[335] Was it a case of Caroline preferring possible financial support provided by having her husband around to the ever-present spectre of the workhouse without him?

330 'Trial of the Prisoners: The Verdict and Sentence", *Coventry Herald*, 18th November 1881.

331 Calendar of Prisoners, 1868-1929: 1881.

332 *Coventry Herald*, 7th October 1881.

333 Registers of Habitual Criminals and Police Gazettes, 1834-1934: 1881-82, Samuel Arnold.

334 On 21st March 1883. Date from 1939 England and Wales Register, which lists Rose as living with her husband John Over and their son John Jr.

335 1885-1948.

The Warders' Hall at Chatham Prison, left, where Oliver Style suffered an accident that would eventually leave him paralysed.

*

Down at Chatham Prison, by 1883 Oliver Style had graduated from working on the docks to being placed in the artisans' yard, where he carried out fitting work and, no doubt bringing great delight and importance to him, looking after all the clocks of the gaol. His expertise in his previous occupation had finally been put to use by the authorities.[336]

Then, the following year, came an incident which would change Oliver's life forever.

The *Coventry Herald and Free Press* reported how

> "While engaged fixing a clock in the Warders' Hall at Chatham, the ladder upon which he was standing slipped at the bottom, causing him to fall heavily. His ankles became swollen, and he

336 Interview with Oliver Style following his release, as reported in the *Coventry Herald and Free Press*, 21st December 1900.

> suffered pain at the bottom of his back. From this fall he never recovered, and two years afterwards he became incapable of work, and did not leave the gaol Infirmary."[337]

Had Henry Jennings read the report, he may have permitted himself a satisfied smile; an eye for an eye, of sorts.

The aftermath of the accident appears to be that Oliver continued to work as best he could; it seems he was initially still able to walk, albeit no doubt in great pain.

The following August he was transferred back to Pentonville, where he spent three months fitting railings before being returned to Chatham on 27th October and carrying out the same task.

Finally, on 13th January 1886, he was admitted to the Infirmary at Chatham Prison, unable to work at all due to his injuries.

On 13th February 1888 Oliver was transferred to Woking Convict Invalid Prison, which had been built in 1859 – as the name suggests – to accommodate invalided inmates,[338] only to be returned to Chatham seven months later on 13th September.[339]

He was increasingly becoming a burden to the system.

337 *Coventry Herald and Free Press*, 21st December 1900. The date of this accident is not recorded.

338 Covering an area of some 63 acres, Woking Gaol was large enough to hold 650 invalided inmates at any one time. It closed in 1889.

339 Interview with Oliver Style following his release, as reported in the *Coventry Herald and Free Press*, 21st December 1900.

8.

THE BIRD SCARER

As Oliver arrived back at his by-now familiar Kent surroundings, at Coventry the catalyst for a double family tragedy was about to occur.

Around the same time as her brother-in-law transferred back to Chatham, Eliza Style – married to his brother Samuel – developed a rheumatic fever, and as her condition worsened she was admitted from their home at 24 Sherbourne Street to the Coventry and Warwickshire Hospital. She died there on 18th November 1888, just thirty-eight years old, with Samuel by her side.[340]

Widowed at forty-two, and with three children,[341] Samuel drifted into severe depression. In the months following Eliza's death he had displayed increasingly strange behaviour; once he had disappeared for some considerable time, and after a long search was discovered lying in a wood. On another occasion he was seen secreting a packet of rat poison, which had to be taken from him before he could inflict any harm to himself.[342]

Eventually it was decided that Samuel should stay for a spell with

340 Death certificate of Eliza Styles, registered 19th November 1888.

341 William (1872-1937), Samuel (1877-1950) and Eliza (1880-1959). A fourth child, also Eliza, was born in 1876 but died the following year. It appears that Matilda and her husband took in their nephews and niece following their father's death; Samuel Jr was still living with them eighteen months later at the time of the 1891 census, while William and Eliza had found work away from home.

342 'Successful at the Third Attempt'. *Warwickshire Herald*, 22nd August 1889.

his sister Matilda, by now married to watchmaker Paul Roby and living with their four children further along the tight community that was Sherbourne Street.

When Samuel's behaviour grew increasingly erratic it was agreed that he would be best served by a spell at the Coventry Union Workhouse Infirmary, where it was hoped a rest would be beneficial. After ten days he appeared to be better, and during a visit from Matilda asked his sister if he could go home. It was a quiet few days at Sherbourne Street, with Samuel seemingly at peace. He carried out small jobs around the house and went for short walks, on one occasion spending a serene afternoon sitting and sharing cigarettes with William Stevens, who kept the gate on Hearsall Common.

Four days later, on Wednesday, 14th August 1889, Samuel once again made his way to the cottage where Stevens was posted while carrying out his duties as gatekeeper.

Matilda saw Samuel leave the house at half-past ten in the morning. The next she heard of him, later that day, was that he was dead.

William Stevens told the inquest held at the Hospital's Committee Room before Coroner Iliffe that he had spent a pleasant enough time chatting with Samuel, and before long they saw a cart coming along the road towards them. As Stevens went over to hold open the gate he heard a loud explosion, and ran as fast as he could back to his hut.

> "Style was lying down with the weapon in front of him, and his shirt near his left side was on fire. Witness put it out, and then found that he was bleeding. Style made no reply when asked why he had interfered with the weapon, which was an old blunderbuss used for frightening birds.[343] Samuel turned his eyes and looked at Stevens. This weapon Stevens said he only loaded with two drachms of power and some paper, but did not use stones or pebbles. Style must have secured the blunderbuss while witness went to open the gate."[344]

343 'Suicide by Shooting with an Old Blunderbuss'. *Coventry Times*, 21st August 1889.

344 *Coventry Standard*, 23rd August 1889.

Hearsall Common.

Police Constable Malin arrived and searched Samuel's clothes, and found a razor in one of his pockets. He arranged for a cab to take him to the hospital, where he was examined by House Surgeon Dr Hewlett, who later told the inquest that when Samuel was admitted

> "he had a circular wound in the chest, and was in a complete state of collapse. [I] made a thorough search of the wound after death, but could find no stones or pebbles. The sixth and seventh ribs were fractured, but [I am] inclined to believe the force of the order would be sufficient to cause the wound if the weapon were placed near to the body."

The jury returned a verdict of Suicide Whilst Temporarily Insane. Coroner Iliffe took the opportunity to comment on how well Samuel had been looked after by his family since he had lost his wife.[345]

*

345 *Coventry Times*, 21st August 1889.

Not included in these words of sympathetic praise was Samuel's elder brother, Oliver Style.

He remained at Chatham for a further two years, in the process serving the first decade of his sentence, and the census of 1891 records him as a 'Convict, married, aged 48'. Tellingly, Harriett told the Coventry enumerator that year that she was a widow.[346]

On 13th November that year Oliver was transferred to Portland Prison,[347] on the Dorset coast. It was originally opened in 1848 as a temporary institution from where prisoners would assist in the construction of the breakwaters at Portland Harbour, much like Chatham Gaol. Nearby homeowners installed cafes in their upper rooms so that curious tourists could watch the prisoners work while enjoying an afternoon tea.[348] The Admiralty Quarries were developed specifically for the convicts to work, and it was estimated that they extracted 10,000 tonnes of stone each week while the breakwater was being constructed.[349]

Presumably not much help at the quarry due to the crippling injuries to his legs, the following year Oliver left Portland for what would be his final transfer, to Parkhurst on the Isle of Wight. He arrived on 7th October 1892,[350] spending the next eight years on the island.

During this time his mother, Maria, died on 26th February 1898 at 1 Spon Causeway,[351] at the incredible age of 92.[352] Given she had seen one son imprisoned and lost two other children to early deaths, it is remarkable that Maria lived to such an advanced age,

346 1891 census return.

347 Interview with Oliver Style following his release, as reported in the *Coventry Herald and Free Press*, 21st December 1900.

348 *Portland Prison Illustrated (1848-2000)* by D.R.G. Legg (2000).

349 Ian West: 'Isle of Portland Quarries – Geology'. University of Southampton.

350 Interview with Oliver Style following his release, as reported in the *Coventry Herald and Free Press*, 21st December 1900.

351 Now Upper Spon Street, which stretches between Allesley Old Road and the corner of Barras Lane.

352 Maria Style was born to Noah and Mary Pearson on 15th September 1806 and baptised at St Dunstan's, Stepney, on 5th October. [Baptismal register].

at a time when a woman's average life expectancy was just above forty.[353]

*

On 14th July 1900, Oliver Style was released early from Parkhurst Prison. He had served twenty of his twenty-five year sentence, and presumably the authorities decided to discharge him rather than have him continue to take up space in the infirmary. He was fifty-seven, and a shadow of his former combative self. A reminder of his violent past was given on his discharge record,[354] which detailed a long list of scars.

Returning to Coventry, the only home he knew outside of prison walls, he was reluctantly taken in by his youngest brother Charles at his home on Yardley Street.[355]

There is no record of any other family member meeting him.[356]

353 'Life expectancy at birth, England and Wales, 1841 to 2011'. Office of National Statistics.

354 Registers of Habitual Criminals and Police Gazettes, 1834-1934: Habitual Criminals Register, 1900.

355 An interview with Oliver Style published in the *Coventry Herald and Free Press* of 21st December 1900 states that on his discharge from prison "for a short time he went to live with his brother in Yardley Street." The 1901 census records Charles Style as a newsagent at 12&13 Yardley Street, living on the premises with wife Ellen and their ten children – the youngest, Katie, being just one month old at the time the census was taken. Charles continued running the newsagent's shop until his death from tuberculosis in September 1907.

356 Many years later, Oliver Style's granddaughter Rita recalled that he had visited following his release to see a newborn grandson, her brother Herbert Charles Style, only to be virtually thrown out of the house when the boy's father, Oliver's son Herbert James Style, returned home. This would seem to indicate the depth of feeling Oliver's family had towards him. See Appendix II.

9.

RETURN OF THE WATCHMAKER

"OLIVER STYLE

On August 5, 1880, Oliver Style, watch finisher, Harnall Row, Far Gosford Street, was committed at Warwick Assizes to penal servitude for 25 years, for a shooting affray, the circumstances of which are, no doubt, in the recollection of many inhabitants. He left gaol on July 14 last,[357] having served but a few days short of twenty years.

He was then practically a cripple, being paralysed in both legs. For a short time he went to live with his brother in Yardley Street; he is now an inmate of the Workhouse Infirmary.

A *Herald* representative, on a visit to the Workhouse this week, looked in at the Infirmary, and found Style busy writing a history of his experiences while in gaol.[358] It appears he has a grievance against the prison authorities, and he is desirous of calling attention to certain treatments to which he was subjected…

Since he returned to Coventry, Style has sent a petition to the Home Secretary, in which he made certain allegations against various prison officials, attributed his crippled condition to neglect, in that the ladder, from which he fell, was not fastened

357 1900.

358 No trace of these memoirs has so far been discovered. The fact Style is reported as writing of his experiences is interesting, given he was unable to sign his own marriage certificate. Was this a misleading description by the newspaper reporter, and Oliver was dictating for a friend to actually write it down, or – more likely – had he received an education while in prison, unable to work through his paralysis?

Oliver Style photographed following his release from prison.
Courtesy Alison Kukla.

at the bottom, and asked for £300 compensation.[359] In reply, the Home Secretary stated that he found no grounds whatever for any action on his part. Style, however, intends to pursue his claim…

Style desires to leave the Workhouse as soon as possible, to return to his old employment – watch-finishing – at which he is confident he could earn his living, despite his paralysis, which has only attacked his legs.

He has a keen, alert face, and his mind is vigorous and active. Altogether he gives the impression of being a man of considerable force of character; a man with plenty of energy and perseverance; one who would not remain long idle if work were found him. He is much better in health than when he left gaol, and is looking forward to the time when he will again take his place among the working men of the city."

Coventry Herald and Free Press,
21st December 1900.

*

Style's pursuit of compensation would not end in victory. He appeared at Coventry Magistrates' Court on 17th December 1900, and asked the Bench for assistance bringing his cause before the public. Telling them he had been "barbarously tortured", he presented a copy of his petition which had been submitted to the Home Secretary. He was told the Secretary of State was the only person who could make any judgment in his case, and that the magistrates had no power to intervene.

Pleading for assistance from the Press, Style was helped from the Court[360] and back to the Coventry Union Workhouse Infirmary on London Road, where he had been admitted just months before.

Despite his good intentions, the watchmaking industry to which he hoped to return was now virtually non-existent. What Oliver couldn't have known was that his incarceration coincided

359 £25,000 in today's money. [National Archives Currency Convertor].
360 *Coventry Herald and Free Press*, 21st December 1900.

with the beginning of the end for the trade; a long, slow decline brought about by competition from Swiss and American watch manufacturers, who offered cheaper timepieces thanks to their automated production lines. Parts made to a standard template were thus interchangeable, resulting in much lower costs.

While this meant a cheaper watch for the end buyer, the quality was not as high as those hand-produced by skilled craftsman and many of Coventry's small businesses and self-employed watchmakers, as Oliver Style had been, refused to adopt the new methods. As a result many went out of business, and in 1894 soup kitchens had appeared in the watchmaking districts to provide help.[361]

An indicator of the drastic decline can be taken from the Coventry Apprentice Registers, which recorded the new apprentices engaged by the city's watchmakers. While the peak year came in 1871, with 239 new apprentices employed, there were still a respectable 101 in 1881, the year after Oliver was convicted. By contrast, the year after his release just nineteen boys entered the trade.[362] Now, on leaving school lads went into the new industries such as of bicycles and motorcars, and associated machine tool manufacturing. Their fathers had learned to adapt their fine-precision skills from watchmaking to these industries, which were to be the next boom for Coventry.

Local historian Mary Montes, in her excellent *Brown Boots in Earlsdon*, evocatively describes the end of the trade:

> 'The watchmaker no longer sat at his bench, eye glass in eye and work in his busy fingers. No longer did he put down his tools mid-morning to wander down his garden to inspect his crop of beans. No longer did he put on his billycock hat to walk down to his master's shop to confer with him about the batch of wheels and pivots brought to him that morning by the errand boy, and then on his way back stand back for a few minutes watching the council workers putting in the new gas lighting in the Lane. The

361 See *Moments in Time: The History of the Coventry Watch Industry Volume 1* by the Coventry Watch Museum Project Limited (5th Edition: 2014).

362 See *Brown Boots in Earlsdon* by Mary Montes (Coventry and Warwickshire Historical Association Pamphlet No. 15) for an excellent examination of the watchmaking trade over the years.

master no longer sat in his little office to enter his transactions in his ledger, or put on his top hat ready to trot down in his pony and trap to his city supplier of jewels, or walk round the corner to the little school to inspect the registers. In the small topshops tools now lay unused on the workbenches, later to be swept aside into loft or garden shed 'out of the way'."[363]

*

Four months after his appearance before the magistrates, when the enumerator arrived on 31st March 1901 to record information for that year's census Oliver was still at the Coventry Workhouse Infirmary, and was subsequently listed as being a pauper inmate, albeit incorrectly as being sixty years old.[364]

Ironically, also resident at the Union at this time was James Styles, the witness to Oliver's triple shooting at the Old Half Moon all those years earlier. He was now fifty-seven years old, and was recorded in the census return as a widowed pauper. He still described himself as a watch case maker.[365] Also in the Union was David Warner, who had helped fix the fatal prize fight between John Plant and Oliver's brother-in-law, Samuel Arnold.[366]

Oliver Style would not leave the workhouse for four more years, and only then in the worst of circumstances.

In that time his two remaining sisters departed this earth; Matilda, who had cared so well for poor Samuel following the passing of his wife, died a painful death at the Coventry and Warwickshire Hospital on 20th December 1903 suffering with colitis and peritonitis.[367] The following year, on 8th June 1904, Caroline died at the Coventry Union Workhouse Infirmary, finally succumbing to necrosis of the skull due to syphilis, which she had

363 Ibid.

364 He was actually fifty-eight.

365 There is no definite record of Mary Ann Styles's death, which occurred some time between the censuses of 1891 and 1901. She may be the 'Marian Styles' recorded in the Death Index for the second quarter of 1898, who died at Croydon, South London, where the couple had lived for a spell.

366 1901 census.

367 Death certificate of Matilda Roby, registered 21st December 1903.

lived with for some years. The disease had, quite literally, destroyed the bones of her skull over a lengthy period of time.[368] One is left to wonder whether she had contracted syphilis from her husband, the despicable Samuel Arnold.

It had been a devastating time. Six months before the death of Caroline, and less than a fortnight after Matilda's demise, Oliver's eldest son Oliver Thomas Style had been admitted to the City Asylum in Birmingham, on New Year's Day 1904.

Oliver Jr had foreseen the collapse of the watchmaking trade and instead turned his attention instead to the cycling industry. At the time of his marriage on 21st September 1890 to Rosa Bates at St Thomas's, the Butts – the same church where his parents had wed – Oliver was working as a turner. They appear to have already welcomed a son, another Oliver, the month before the happy event,[369] and a daughter, Nora, soon followed in 1892. Another daughter arrived on 19th October 1893, but Rosa was severely ill as she went into labour, having been stricken with typhoid fever for four weeks before the birth, and following the arrival was confined to her room but died on 1st November 1893, aged just twenty-two.[370] The newborn was named after her mother.

Oliver found happiness again six years later, when he married Elizabeth Roberts. In the 1901 census the couple were recorded at Ivetsey Place, Aston, with Oliver Jr, Nora and Rosa Jr. Their father was working as a cycle tool maker.

At this stage, life looked good for the young family. Yet, as so often seems to be the case in the Style story, within a few years fate intervened yet again. On 1st January 1904 Oliver Jr was admitted to the City Asylum, Birmingham. He was three weeks shy of his thirty-seventh birthday. He would remain at the asylum for just over a year before expiring on 9th January 1905.[371]

The reason for his admission is unknown, but the death certificate

368 Death certificate of Caroline Arnold, registered 8th June 1904.
369 Oliver Style was born on 28th August 1890.
370 Death certificate of Rosa Style, registered 2nd November 1893.
371 Lunacy Patients Admission Registers, 1846-1912. Piece 39: 1904.

gives the cause as 'General Paralysis'. His widow, Elizabeth, notified the registrar the following day.[372]

It was not the first time that a member of the family had died in such an institution. On 26th June 1856 Robert Style – brother of Oliver Style's father John – had been admitted to Hanwell Insane Asylum in West London, where he died the following month, on 21st July.[373] And it would not be the last.

After Hanwell Asylum had been opened in 1831 to accommodate London's insane as the First Middlesex County Asylum, the government ordered that more such facilities be built around the country and passed the 1845 County Asylums Act. Colney Hatch in north London became the Second Middlesex County Asylum in 1851, and the following year a facility for the inhabitants of Warwickshire was opened at Hatton.

As the Warwick County Lunatic Asylum it occupied grounds initially of forty-two acres, eventually increasing to over three hundred, and at one point accommodating over 1,500 patients.

By modern standards treatment was harsh, including electric shock therapy, but life at Hatton was in the main of a more comfortable nature than the private asylums, or older facilities less concerned with the welfare of patients.[374]

It was to Hatton Asylum that William Bruce, a sixty-eight year old labourer, was sent. He had been an inmate of the Warwick Union Workhouse, but apparently through drink had become mentally unstable. The Union's Head Nurse Caroline Perrett reported that

> "He is very violent, striking at nurses and attendants. Refuses food, is restless constantly, getting out of bed, crawling under bed, on the floor. His speech is confused. He sleeps but little. Very dirty in his habits."

Dr Frank Gardner agreed, and recommended that William be

372 Death certificate of Oliver Thomas Style, dated 10th January 1905.

373 Lunacy Patients Admission Registers, 1846-1912. Piece 16: May 1855 – December 1858.

374 www.countyasylums.co.uk/central-hospital-hatton. The hospital became part of the NHS in 1948, and eventually closed in July 1995.

sent to Hatton, where he was admitted on 14th August 1903.[375]

The next new arrival, four days later, was Oliver Style, who became inmate 7627.

He had been at the Infirmary at the Coventry Union Workhouse for more than two years, and had been examined there on 14th August 1903 by Dr Charles Webb Iliffe – the coroner who had presided over the inquest into the suicide of Oliver's brother Samuel fourteen years earlier – and declared a 'person of unsound mind'.

The Statement of Particulars on his admission form recorded that Oliver was sixty-two years old – incorrectly adding two years to his correct age – and that he was married, although his wife's address was not known. This, his first attack, had lasted for several months, and he was both suicidal and a danger to others, being 'very violent'.

The detailed notes by Dr Iliffe reveal Oliver's state of mind – and the cause, which echoes his interview with the *Coventry Herald and Free Press* upon his release from prison:

> "He has a delusion that his letters & writings are taken away & withheld from him. He spends all his time on writing his sad fate; he sends letter after letter to the Lord Chief Justice, the Prison authorities & the press that he is being tortured & that he deserves some one to shoot him.
>
> He has finished a sentence of 21 years penal servitude for shooting 4 or 5 people.[*sic*]'

A nurse at the Union Workhouse Infirmary, Mary Whale,[376] gave her opinion, which was also recorded on the admission form:

> "I have watched & caused to have Style watched by other nurses.

375 Warwickshire County Record Office: CR 1664/351/1-2 (No. 7621: William Bruce).

376 Many years later, Oliver Style's granddaughter Rita – born the year before his release from prison – recalled that she had been told that her grandfather had gone to live in London with a nurse 'from the prison', but this could well be a story told to explain Oliver's subsequent 'disappearance' from the family. See Appendix II. Mary Whale was born on 25th August 1865 and began working at the Coventry Union Workhouse before the 1891 census. In the 1911 return she was recorded as the Superintendent Nurse in the Workhouse. She died in July 1940 aged seventy-four.

The Lodge at Hatton Asylum.

> He is at times very excited. Has struck a man on the head with a stick in the hospital & [says] that all the inmates & nurses are spies & desire to send him to a mad home. When not excited he remains in bed and will take no food & [is] very sullen. His vitality is going down by reason of his not eating food & worrying."[377]

Despite the best efforts of Hatton's Medical Superintendent Alfred Miller[378] and his medical team, and close monitoring by the Asylum staff, Oliver 'Cromwell' Style declined steadily and died

377 Warwickshire County Record Office: CR 1664/351/1-2 (No. 7626: Oliver Style).

378 Alfred Miller was educated at Trinity College, Dublin and graduated in 1881. He was connected with Hatton Asylum for forty years, first as Assistant Medical Officer and then serving as Medical Superintendent for thirty-four years until his death in December 1923. He held a number of other posts in Warwickshire, including that of Medical Advisor of the County Mental Deficiency Act Committee. Obituary in the *British Medical Journal*, 29th December 1923.

two years later, on Saturday, 21st October 1905, at 11.25 in the evening. Present was Ernest Prestwich, the Head Night Attendant.

A post mortem revealed death had been from an abscess of the lung from which Oliver had been suffering for three months, caused by 'Chronic mania'. There were no unusual circumstances.[379]

The Notice of Death was certified by Superintendent Miller, who also registered the event on 8th November 1905.[380]

As a final mark of their feelings towards him, the family refused to accept Oliver's body for burial in Coventry,[381] and he was interred in the cemetery grounds at Hatton Lunatic Asylum on 26th October 1905, with no marker.[382]

So ended the life of the author of the so-called 'Murderous Outrage in Coventry'.

The watchmaker was dead.

379 Warwickshire County Record Office: CR 1664/516 (Notices of Deaths of Patients). Forename of Ernest Prestwich from 1901 census.

380 Death certificate of Oliver Style, registered on 8th November 1905.

381 See Appendix II.

382 Warwickshire County Record Office: CR 1664/551 (Register of Burials at the Asylum).

10.

QUEEN OF THE CASTLE

While few shed a tear for the passing of Oliver Style, the family which he had apparently loved yet had hurt so badly continued with their lives while he was detained at Her Majesty's Pleasure.

Ann Elkington, his mother-in-law, had not been expected to survive her injuries. Yet her wounds healed, and in April the following year, as the 1881 census was taken, she was still living on Much Park Street, but now at No. 20. Husband Thomas was recorded as a lodger in Bacup, Lancashire.

Ann eventually passed away on 5th September 1888, aged seventy-seven, at 14 Court 3 House Much Park Street, the cause given as 'Senile Decay' on the death certificate. The informant was her husband Thomas,[383] who by 1891 was living alone at 19 Court 4 House Much Park Street.[384] Obviously struggling to cope on his own, Thomas eventually moved in with his daughter Ann and her family at their home at 47 Moor Street, Earlsdon, and was recorded there in the 1901 census. He died three months later of 'Senile phthisis' – tuberculosis – and exhaustion. He was ninety years old.[385]

Ann and Thomas's grandson Arthur, who was two years old and staying at their home on Much Park Street as Harriett sought refuge from the violent Oliver, had suffered a wound to his forehead from a bullet fired by his father which glanced off his skull. The

383 Death certificate of Ann Elkington, registered on 6th September 1888.
384 1891 census.
385 Death certificate of Thomas Elkington, registered 31st July 1901.

census taken the following year reveals that Harriett had moved her children to Harnall Place,[386] and ten years later they were at Abbott's Lane, with the then thirteen year old Arthur employed doing bicycle work.[387] The following March Arthur was baptised at Holy Trinity, now aged fourteen. Interestingly, perhaps for the sake of respectability more than anything, Harriett had made sure that his father's name appeared on the baptism record.[388]

On 24th September 1898 Arthur married Alice Clarke. He was still forging a career in the bicycle industry, living on Trafalgar Street, and his bride lived with her family at 6 Nelson Street.[389]

Three years later the young couple had moved to Middlemore Place, off Wellesley Street in Birmingham.[390] Over the next decade, life was good for Arthur and Alice. He had become an experienced cycle liner and enameller, and the couple welcomed children Stanley,[391] Edward,[392] Alice[393] and Jennie.[394] In April 1911, as the census was taken, the family were living at 56 Wellesley Street.

Yet this was a period of political unrest around the world, following power struggles across Europe and a number of conflicts which led to the outbreak of the First World War in 1914. Having demanded that Germany comply with the 1839 Treaty of London which specified that Belgium must remain neutral, but receiving no reply by the deadline of 11.00pm on 4th August, the British Empire was at war with Germany.

It did not take long for new recruits to be needed to bolster the regular army. Like most regiments across the country, the Royal Warwickshire encouraged local men to volunteer into what was known as 'Kitchener's Army', and the 14th, 15th and 16th (Service)

386 1881 census.
387 1891 census.
388 Baptism records of Arthur Edward Style.
389 Marriage certificate of Arthur Edward Style and Alice Jane Clarke.
390 1901 census.
391 1904-1979.
392 1906-1973.
393 Born 1908.
394 1910–1987.

Battalions were raised in September 1914 from men volunteering in Birmingham, becoming known as 'the Birmingham Pals'.[395] One of them was Arthur Edward Style, who had enlisted into the 11th Battalion as Private 10155, and then transferred to the 14th to be with his 'Pals'.[396]

After a period of training and drill, the battalions were moved to France for service on the Western Front, landing at Boulogne-sur-Mer as part of the 95th Brigade in the 32nd Division in November 1915.

At the Chantilly Conference the following month, the Allies decided upon a strategy of combined offensives to take place in 1916, with the intention of hastening an Allied victory and an end to the War. The British and French committed themselves to an offensive centred around a river in northern France – the Somme. The British troops were made up of a combination of the pre-war army, the Territorial Force and Kitchener's Army, the wartime volunteers.

On the first day of the Battle of the Somme almost 20,000 British soldiers were killed, with another 37,500 wounded. Many of them were from the Pals regiments, seeing their first action on the most bloody day in British military history.

The so-called Second Phase, from July to September 1916, started with the Allies attempting to capture the village of Longueval, in what became known as the Battle of Delville Wood.

General Sir Henry Rawlinson's plan was to advance across No-Man's Land at night for a dawn attack, but Field Marshal Douglas Haig disagreed, having doubts about the inexperienced New Army divisions assembling on the battlefield at night. After modifications to the plan Haig assented. But he was right to be concerned.

On 30th July attacks were made at Delville Wood and Longueval, with a preliminary bombardment starting at 4.45pm failing to

395 See *Birmingham Pals: 14th, 15th & 16th (Service) Battalions of the Royal Warwickshire Regiment, A History of the Three City Battalions Raised in Birmingham in World War One* by Terry Carter (2012).

396 WWI Service Medal and Award Rolls, 1914-1920: Arthur E. Style.

AREN'T THEY WORTH
DEFENDING?
JOIN THE VOLUNTEERS
AND BE READY
WARWICKSHIRE VOLUNTEER REGIMENT.
1st BATTALION.
Battalion Headquarters—WITTON BARRACKS.
COMPANY HEADQUARTERS:
"A" Coy.—Drill Hall, Soho Road, HANDSWORTH.
"B" Coy.— " " "
"C" Coy.—Council House, SUTTON COLDFIELD.
"D" Coy.—104, Colmore Row, BIRMINGHAM.
4th BATTALION.
Battalion Headquarters—STONEY LANE BARRACKS.
COMPANY HEADQUARTERS:
"A" Coy. (Harborne)—The Drill Hall, HARBORNE.
"B" Coy. (Moseley)—The Drill Hall, Stoney Lane, SPARKBROOK.
"C" Coy. (Rotton Park)—145, DUDLEY ROAD.
"D" Coy. (Balsall Heath)—The Drill Hall, Stoney Lane, SPARKBROOK.
5th BATTALION.
Battalion Headquarters—WITTON BARRACKS.
COMPANY HEADQUARTERS:
"A" Coy.—The Old Skating Rink, Village Green, ERDINGTON.
"B" Coy.—586, Coventry Road, SMALL HEATH.
"C" Coy.—WITTON BARRACKS.
" Coy.—Metropolitan Wagon & Carriage Works, Y.
PERCIVAL JONES LTD, PRINTERS, BIRM

suppress the German artillery, which fired heavily on the village and the wood.

Further attempts were made, but under constant German artillery fire the Allies withdrew, having suffered many casualties.

One of these was Private Arthur Style. His body was never found, and his military record was marked 'Death presumed'.[397]

As such, he is one of the 72,337 British and South African men listed on the Thiepval Memorial to the Missing of the Somme, which records those with no known grave who died at the Battle of the Somme.[398]

On 30th March 1917 his widow Alice was awarded a pension of £24 6s, later increased to £31 3s and £39 2s;[399] but it didn't compensate for the loss of her husband, who started his life under gunfire and ended it the same way.

Arthur's surviving siblings,[400] in the main, enjoyed long and happy lives except, as we have heard, eldest brother Oliver Thomas Style. Following his appearance as a witness for the defence at his father's committal hearing, Oliver Jr began working as an iron turner,[401] and by the time of his marriage to Rosa Bates in September 1890 was employed as a machinist, living at Moat Street.[402] A son, another Oliver, had been born a month earlier.[403]

The following year Oliver was plying his trade in Coventry's burgeoning cycle industry,[404] and in 1892 the family welcomed a daughter, Nora. 1893 brought joy and tragedy: Rosa Jr was born,[405] but days later her mother passed away.[406]

Oliver would remain a widower for six years, until in May 1899

397 Army Registers of Soldiers' Effects, 1901-1929: Arthur Edward Style.
398 Arthur Style's name is inscribed on Pier and Face 9A 9B and 10B.
399 WWI Pension Ledgers and Index Cards, 1914-1923: Arthur Edward Style.
400 Sisters Edith Annie and Rhoda had died in infancy.
401 1881 census.
402 Marriage certificate of Oliver Style and Rosa Bates.
403 Date of birth from 1939 Register.
404 1891 census.
405 Born 19th October 1893.
406 Rosa Style died on 1st November 1893.

he married Elizabeth Roberts at St Jude's, Birmingham.[407] The family stayed in the area, and are recorded in the 1901 census at Wellesley Street, Aston, with Oliver now employed as a cycle tool maker. Following the shock of losing Rosa all seemed to be looking up for Oliver, but just three years later he was admitted to the City Asylum on Lodge Road, Birmingham.[408] He never came out. On 10th January 1905 Elizabeth reported the death of her husband, which had occurred the previous day. The cause was recorded as 'General Paralysis' – what had prompted such a mental decline? There is a suggestion that the term 'general paralysis' of the insane is a severe neuropsychiatric disorder, a result of late-stage syphilis. We don't know what Oliver's wellbeing was like between 1901 and 1904 – could he have been displaying symptoms in the lead up to his admittance to the asylum?

Edith Harriett Style, at school when her father was sent to gaol, was working as a silk weaver by the 1891 census. She is recorded as still living with the family on Abbott's Lane, but four months later married machinist James Lapworth.[409] Eight children were born to the couple: Edith,[410] Emily,[411] Horace,[412] Herbert,[413] Redvers,[414] Ida,[415] Hilda[416] and Frank.[417] Edith died in 1953, aged eighty-four.[418]

Also at school in 1880 was Elizabeth, then aged ten.[419] On 16th February 1889 she married Alpha Lewis[420] at Coventry's Holy Trinity, a twenty-three year old engineer living on Spon Street.[421] A

407 Marriage certificate of Oliver Thomas Style and Elizabeth Roberts.
408 On 1st January 1904.
409 Marriage certificate gives the wedding date as 15th August 1891.
410 1892-1978.
411 1894-1982.
412 1895-1955.
413 1897-1979.
414 1900-1976.
415 1902-1986.
416 1904-1964.
417 1910-1983.
418 England & Wales, Death Index, 1916-2007: Edith H. Lapworth.
419 1881 census.
420 1866-1918.

son, William, died in infancy the following summer.[422]

By the time of the 1891 census, taken on 5th April, the couple were living at 14 Court, 3 House, Much Park Street – the house where Elizabeth's grandmother Ann Elkington had died in 1888. Had they been living with her in her final days? A son, Alpha James Lewis,[423] was born there on 18th November 1891.[424] His father, Alpha Sr, was now working as a cycle fitter,[425] illustrating the move from watchmaking to the cycle industry over this period for much of Coventry's workforce.

Daughters Doris[426] and Madge[427] joined the family, followed by another son, Fred,[428] by which time the Lewises had moved to Birmingham. They settled into what would be the long-standing family home at 67 Bordesley Green Road, Saltley, being recorded there in the 1911 census and the 1939 Register. During this time Alpha passed away, in 1918, leaving widow Elizabeth on her own for a further thirty-six years. She died on 25th November 1954, aged eighty-three, leaving her effects to son Fred.[429]

Herbert James Style[430] was just seven when his father was sent to prison. It is believed within the family he was made to leave Bablake School, where he was a pupil, as a result of the disgrace brought to the family.[431]

By 1891 he was working in the cycle industry,[432] and seven years later, at the time of his marriage, was a clerk for a cycle works company. The couple evidently met through work, as Herbert's

421 Marriage certificate of Alpha William Lewis and Elizabeth Jane Style.
422 FreeBMD Death Index, 1837-1915: William Lewis (Q3 1890).
423 1891-1960.
424 Baptismal register of Alpha James Lewis.
425 Ibid.
426 1895-1963.
427 1898-1986.
428 1905-1996.
429 Probate record of Elizabeth Jane Lewis, dated 10th December 1954.
430 Known as 'Burton' within the family.
431 Notes from a conversation between Herbert's daughter-in-law Doris Style and her son Derek c1985.
432 1891 census.

bride was Rose Moss,[433] a cycle valve stamper. Like Herbert, Rose's father was a watch maker.[434]

A daughter, Marguerite, was born on 20th March 1899,[435] and son Herbert Charles arrived in December the following year.[436] Norman completed the family in January 1904.[437]

At the time of the 1911 census the family were living on Villiers Street, with Herbert Sr working as a screw gauge maker at a motor car works, and in 1939 he was a jig and tool maker.[438]

For a long time struggling with asthma, Herbert moved the family to Sharnford in Leicestershire for the cleaner air. He smoked menthol cigarettes, thinking they were good for him, and slept in a leather armchair in the parlour instead of going to bed, no doubt finding it easier to sleep sitting up.[439] He died on 11th February 1944 of heart disease and asthma.[440]

Youngest surviving child Florence, born in December 1875, was working as a watch jewel hole maker by 1891.[441] She married Norman Tanner[442] on 18th September 1897,[443] a draughtsman,[444] and the couple moved north to Yorkshire by the time their son Norman Jr[445] was born the following year at Leeds. Daughter Gladys[446] was there on 24th January 1900.

Norman Sr and Florence returned to the Midlands by the 1939 Register, being recorded at 6 Wallace Road, Loughborough, and

433 1879-1956. It is said Rose had a beautiful singing voice. See Appendix II.
434 Marriage certificate of Herbert James Style and Rose Beatrice Moss, 29th January 1898.
435 Marguerite Rose Style, known as 'Slap', 1899-1987. See Appendix II.
436 Herbert Charles Style, known as 'Rogue', 1900-1960.
437 Norman Style, known as 'Spug', 1904-1984.
438 1939 Register.
439 Family recollections.
440 Death certificate of Herbert James Style, registered 12th February 1944.
441 1891 census.
442 Norman William Henry Tanner, 1877-1939.
443 Style family Bible.
444 1901 and 1911 census returns, 1939 Register.
445 1898-1989.
446 1900-1990.

Norman died there on 9th December that year.[447] Florence followed twenty years later, on 12th December 1959, aged eighty-three.[448]

*

What of their mother, Harriett?

Having escaped from her husband's violence, she set about raising her children. In the census taken the year after his incarceration, Harriett is recorded as undertaking ribbon weaving at Harnall Place, off Robinson Row, with Edith, Elizabeth, Herbert, Florence all at school, along with three-year-old Arthur relying on her to support them. Eldest Oliver Jr was doing his bit, working as an iron turner.[449]

In 1891 the family were at Abbott's Lane, with Harriett still weaving and the children now all employed.[450]

By the turn of the 1900s, however, everything had changed. All the children had left home, and Harriett, now fifty-four, was living alone – albeit with two women lodgers. But instead of taking in weaving work, she was now running the Castle Stores grocery shop at 25 Castle Street, Hillfields.[451] Ten years later she was still there,[452] no doubt earning a decent living and enjoying the respectability which came with it.

As is always the case at such shops, the cornerstone of the community, Harriett no doubt enjoyed the opportunity to tittle-tattle that seeing the same friendly faces each day brought. Did she, perhaps, welcome the chance to bask a little in the glow of the notorious events of thirty years earlier?[453]

447 Probate record for Norman William Henry Tanner, dated 17th February 1940.
448 Date of Florence's death taken from joint grave.
449 1881 census.
450 1891 census.
451 1901 census.
452 1911 census.
453 According to a conversation between Doris Style, the wife of Harriett's grandson Norman, and her son Derek which took place around 1985, Harriett was a workhorse, and very chatty.

The Castle Stores next door to the Elephant and Castle.

How had this transformation in her fortunes occurred?

According to Rita Style, Harriett's granddaughter[454] who was close to her, the shop had been bought for Harriett by her 'fancy man' who ran the pub next door to the Castle Stores.[455] This was the Elephant and Castle at No. 23, where from 1890 the landlord was Thomas Bates, who gave up the licence upon the death of his wife Lydia in 1903. After that it was run by Richard Weaver, still recorded there in the 1911 census.[456] It doesn't seem likely that the admirer was Thomas Bates, who had just turned thirty and raising a young family when Harriett probably took over the Castle Stores.

Perhaps a better clue lies in the 1891 census, which shows the landlord of the Hare and Hounds at 32 Castle Street as being Henry Hewitt, a forty year old widower with six young children.

454 Marguerite 'Rita' Style (1899-1987) was the daughter of Herbert James Style, second son of Harriett and Oliver.

455 See Appendix II.

456 Business directories; census returns; Directory of Deaths: Lydia Bates.

His wife Elizabeth had died the previous year.[457] Ten years later Henry was still running the Hare and Hounds,[458] now with a wife, Ann.[459] We don't know when Harriett began running the Castle Stores, but it must have been some point in the 1890s. Had she and Henry become close in the years before he met Ann?

At some point after the 1911 census Harriett moved into two adjoining cottages on Nelson Street, where a brother had several properties.[460]

She developed cataracts and in time was registered blind,[461] no doubt a savage blow to such a hard worker. She employed a housekeeper, who was gifted the cottages[462] after Harriett's death on 5th April 1929, aged eighty-three. She was buried in Coventry's London Road Cemetery four days later.[463]

There can be no doubt that many more people attended her funeral than witnessed the interment of her husband a quarter of a century earlier.

457 Death Index, 1890: Elizabeth Hewitt.
458 Later renumbered to 60 Castle Street.
459 1901 census.
460 Probably Walter Elkington (1850-1941). Harriett's other brothers were James, who had died in 1892, and Thomas, who had moved to Wales by 1891 and died there in 1901. Walter lived at Upper Nelson Street in 1891, and at 57 Castle Street in 1901, when Harriett was at No. 25.
461 Notes from a conversation between Doris Style, who married Harriett's grandson Norman, and her son Derek c1985.
462 According to her granddaughter Rita, who had originally been left the cottages by Harriett. See Appendix II.
463 Warwickshire Burial Records, FindMyPast.com

CONCLUSION

"TIME BRINGS CHANGES"

There is a lot of sadness, and little happiness, in the story of the watchmaker's revenge. Yet, despite the actions of Oliver Style being utterly deplorable, it has to be said that many of the events described in this book were the result of the time during which the participants lived.

Any city or large town in the Victorian era – not just Coventry – struggled with overcrowding, poor sanitation and poverty, which led more often than not to crime and drunkenness, which in turn, sadly, resulted in domestic abuse. Infant mortality across the country was high; in 1865, the year Oliver and Harriett Style welcomed their first child, 266 children out of every thousand died before their fifth birthday – more than one in four.[464] And the Styles certainly had their own experience of this, losing both Edith and Rhoda at a tender age.

Yet Coventry had something which many cities did not; industry so uniquely concentrated that the vast majority of its population was able to find employment within the same trade, firstly weaving then watchmaking, and bicycles and motorcars into the twentieth century. There was relatively little unemployment, and, in the case of the watchmaking industry, a structured hierarchy which allowed even schoolboys to put their first step on the ladder which could

464 'Child mortality in the United Kingdom 1800-2020' available at www.statista.com/statistics/1041714/united-kingdom-all-time-child-mortality-rate.

see them rise to be their own boss, highly-skilled and always in demand. Coventry always gave its own opportunities.

And this is exactly what happened in the case of Alice Arnold, born in the Coventry Union Workhouse to Caroline five months after Oliver Style had been imprisoned.[465] She would never know her uncle, but his actions surely in time provided Alice with a determination, along with her own early experiences.

With her father Samuel Arnold seemingly unable – or unwilling – to take care of his family, Caroline and her children Emma (six years old), Mary Ann (four) and Robert (two) had entered the workhouse at the end of 1880, and Alice was born there on 19th January the following year.

Mother and children were still there when the census was taken on 3rd April 1881, and the return for the Coventry Union Workhouse reveals there were 388 souls seeking refuge at that time.

In fact, they would not be discharged for nearly another year, finally passing out of the facility's doors on 19th February 1882 – fourteen months after they entered. As we have seen, three months later they were reconciled with Samuel following his release from prison. The family settled into rooms in the squalid Chauntry Place as Samuel and Caroline scrabbled for paying work, and two more children were soon added to the family.

Poverty stricken, the children did their bit. By the age of sixteen Emma was working as a cotton filler,[466] and had almost certainly been employed for several years before that. She married William Morris five years later, in 1896, no doubt taking the first opportunity to escape the desperate situation.[467] Sister Mary Ann Arnold married coal merchant George Nickols in 1901 and had five children.[468] According to historian Cathy Hunt, in her excellent

465 See page 87.
466 1891 census.
467 On 22nd March 1896 at Holy Trinity, Coventry. The couple had eight children who survived into adulthood. Emma died in 1949.
468 1911 census. Mary Ann died in 1946.

biography of Alice Arnold,[469] family information states that Robert Arnold joined the army and lost his life in the Boer War.

Alice began her working life at the age of just eleven, being employed in factory work.[470] and by twenty was working in the cycle industry as a packer.[471]

It was around this time that Caroline became bedridden[472] due to the syphilis from which she had been suffering. It seems likely that she was cared for by her daughters – Alice would later reply, when asked why she loved Coventry, "It was the birthplace of the one I dearly love, my mother."[473] – before Caroline was admitted to the Coventry Union Workhouse Infirmary, where she died on 8th June 1904.[474]

When father Samuel died two years later[475] it's unlikely he was held in such affection.

By 1909 Alice was a member of the Social Democratic Federation, Britain's first organised socialist political party initially founded in 1894 in London, and acted as the first Secretary of the Coventry Branch's Women's Circle. At a time when increased numbers of women were finding work in the nation's factories, the Federation sought to recruit them to their socialist principles, and the Women's Circle gave them the opportunity to discuss the issues they faced.

When the Great War started and Coventry's workers, as with those all around the country, found themselves under pressure from factory bosses to cope with increased production for the war effort, Alice was employed at the Rudge Whitworth cycle factory on Spon Street which was commandeered by the government to produce ammunition and other military items. This inevitably saw

469 Cathy Hunt: *A Woman of the People: Alice Arnold of Coventry 1881–1955* (Coventry and County Heritage Series Booklet No. 27) by Cathy Hunt (2007).
470 Kenneth Richardson, *Twentieth Century Coventry* (1972).
471 1901 census.
472 Family information quoted in Cathy Hunt's *A Woman of the People: Alice Arnold of Coventry 1881–1955*.
473 *Coventry Evening Telegraph*, 22nd January 1945.
474 Death certificate of Caroline Arnold, registered 8th June 1904.
475 In Autumn 1906.

an increase in the number of working class women being employed. Alice was a shop steward, and as such encouraged female workers at the factory to join the Workers' Union.

In 1917 she was appointed the union's women's organiser for the Coventry area, a position which brought with it a full-time wage. It was a role which she carried out with distinction for fourteen years, representing thousands of women. In the process she had been elected onto Coventry City Council in 1919 as the Worker's Union candidate, and became one of Coventry's first two female councillors alongside the Labour candidate, Ellen Hughes. Alice would serve on the council for thirty-six years.

From the start, Alice's focus was on better living and work conditions for the poorer families of the city, as a result becoming a much respected figure. In 1928 she joined the Labour party, strengthening her majority.

Between 1931 and 1934 she was Chair of the Public Health Committee, which was responsible for the slum clearance programme which saw the demolition of many of the streets she had known in her childhood and which have been described in this book, including Much Park Street.

She was elected Mayor of Coventry in November 1937 – the first woman to be awarded the role.[476]

Covering the election result, the *Midland Daily Telegraph* carried the speech given by the new Mayor:

> "'Time brings changes in its course and a great change has come to Coventry at this moment,' was a passage in the speech of Miss Alderman Arnold – Coventry's first woman, in the 589 years since Coventry was incorporated, to occupy the Mayoral Chair – in returning thanks for the honour bestowed upon her today.
>
> The new Mayor, who was born and bred in the city and who had served just over 18 years on the City Council, said she realised that the present juncture was one of particularly acute difficulty.

476 See *A Woman of the People: Alice Arnold of Coventry 1881-1955* (Coventry and County Heritage Series Booklet No. 27) by Cathy Hunt (2007) and *A History of Women's Lives in Coventry* by Cathy Hunt (2018) for a full and insightful account of the life of this important woman in Coventry's history.

'All I want to say is this,' said the Mayor. 'That while many will doubtless regard the change as good and many others as bad, I trust they will recognise beneath their differences of opinion that all are united in the desire to promote the well-being of this city, which has had so great a past, and will, we all believe, have an even greater future. I hope there will be sportsmanship on both sides, that the change will be accepted in good part, and that I shall receive the united support of the Council and the public.

'I have received messages of congratulation from many quarters - one in particular has touched me very much,' said the Mayor. 'It is from our old and revered friend, Colonel Wyley, who is prevented by illness from being present. In his touching note the Colonel says: 'I know that you will do your utmost for the honour of the city we both dearly love, and you will be helped by a very charming lady - Mrs Alderman Hughes - and the result will be, I feel sure, a very happy and prosperous year."

Mentioning that she was the first woman in the history of Coventry to occupy the Mayoral chair, the Mayor said she believed, whatever their party or creed, this fact would be a source of satisfaction to the women of Coventry who would rejoice in this recognition of the rights of their sex.

'Women have no wish for domination and no desire for anything in the nature of sex antagonism,' remarked the Mayor. 'But they do feel that in these modern times the recognition of their right to stand side by side with men in the work of the world is a great and important principle. The liberties of the citizens of Coventry began with the sacrifice of a woman - the great Lady Godiva - and George Eliot - one of the greatest of women novelists - was born just outside the city and was nurtured in the city. Apart altogether from any question of the merits of a particular holder of the office it is in accordance with the tradition of Coventry that the high office of mayoralty should be declared open to women.'[477]

*

477 *Midland Daily Telegraph*, 9th November 1937.

Alice Arnold, first woman Mayor of Coventry.

If there is one good thing to have emerged from the whole sorry tale of Oliver Style and his actions, it is the inspiring determination to learn from her humble roots and commitment to the cause of women's rights displayed by Alice Arnold.

Today, with women still campaigning for parity of wages and an end to domestic violence, sexism and misogyny – the same struggles faced by Alice's mother Caroline and all women of that era – it is shameful that, more than one hundred and forty years after the birth of the remarkable Alice Arnold, these issues are still with us.

APPENDIX I

TIMELINE OF OLIVER STYLE

1843
19th January: Born at Bethnal Green. Family move to Coventry.

1859
23rd November: In court charged with assaulting Susannah Sankey.

1861
Census: at Bromsgrove Street, Birmingham.

1862
27th October: Charged with assaulting William Bradshaw.

1864
1st August: Married Harriett Elkington.
25th November: Charged with assaulting Abraham Knight.

1865
22nd February: Birth of daughter Edith Annie.

1867
21st January: Birth of son Oliver Thomas.

1868
3rd August: Death of daughter Edith Annie.
30th November: Birth of daughter Edith Harriett.

1870
24th May: Assaulted Abraham Knight on Spon End.
27th November: Birth of daughter Elizabeth Jane.

1871
Census: at 84 Craven Street.

1872
15th June: Birth of daughter Rhoda.

1873
25th December: Birth of son Herbert James.

1874
11th March: Charged with a Breach of contract.

1875
30th December: Birth of daughter Florence.

1876
12th April: Charged with non-maintenance of an illegitimate child.

1877
2nd January: Death of daughter Rhoda.
1st December: Birth of son Arthur Edward.

1879
Summer: Rows with Harriett about White and Goddard.

1880
27th April: Disagreement at the Liberal Ball.
5th May: The couple separate, Harriett moves in with her mother.
26th May: Oliver Jr goes to ask their mother to come home.
27th May: Between six and seven that evening buys a revolver in Birmingham. At 9.10pm enters the Old Half Moon and shoots Henry Jennings, James Pallett and Maria Feltham. At 9.30pm arrives at Much Park Street and shoots Harriett, Ann Elkington and son Arthur.
29th May: Remanded.
12th July: Committal hearing.
4th August: Trial at Warwick Summer Assizes.
5th August: Sentenced to 25 years' imprisonment.
26th August: Taken to Pentonville Prison.

1881
28th March: Transferred to Chatham.

1884
Falls from a ladder, severely injuring his legs.

1885
???? August: Transferred back to Pentonville.
27th October: Returned to Chatham.

1886
13th January: Admitted to the Infirmary at Chatham Prison, unable to work at all due to his injuries.

1888
13th February: Transferred to the Infirmary at Woking Gaol.

1891
Census: 'Convict, married, aged 48'.
13th November: Transferred to Portland Prison.

1892
7th October: Transferred to Parkhurst, Isle of Wight.

1900
14th July: Released after serving 20 years. Goes to stay with brother Charles at his home on Yardley Street. Around August is admitted to the Coventry Union Workhouse, writes to the Home Secretary.
17th December: Before magistrates seeking assistance.

1901
   Census: at the Coventry Union Workhouse Infirmary.
1903
   18th August Admitted to Hatton Lunatic Asylum.
1905
   21st October: Dies of 'Chronic mania'.
   26th October: Buried in grounds of Hatton Asylum.

APPENDIX II

MEMORIES OF AUNT RITA

In the early 1980s Derek and Pat Style, keen family genealogists, recorded a conversation with Derek's aunt Marguerite Rose Style (Rita), who had been born in 1899 and had memories of her grandfather – Oliver Style – but more especially of her grandmother, Harriett, with whom she was close.

I'm grateful to Derek and Pat's daughter Alison for the transcript of this conversation, and permission to publish it here. Given she was in her early eighties at the time it's understandable that Rita misremembered the odd detail. She died on 20th September 1987.

*

(Derek and Pat have visited Rita at her home. They are looking at a photograph).

Derek: So there's three children along the back. That's Gran Style…[478]

478 Rose Beatrice Moss (1879-1956), wife of Oliver Style's son Herbert James Style and Rita's mother.

Rita: There's Amy,[479] there's Elsie,[480] Dad.[481]

Derek: My Dad[482] used to talk about Edie.[483]

Rita: Yes, there was aunt Edith and aunt Elizabeth.[484] She wouldn't allow you to call her Lizzie. 'Elizabeth', you'd got to call her. She was a bee up the vacuum, a real so-and-so. There were four children. There was Oliver,[485] Dad, aunt Edith and aunt Elizabeth.[486]

Derek: And who was the oldest?

Rita: Dad. Your uncle Oliver's dead and Edith's dead.

Derek: But what I mean is who was the oldest son. Was it your father?

Rita: Dad, yes.[487]

Derek: Was he born in Coventry?

Rita: Yes.

Derek: Do you know where?

Rita: My grandfather[488] shot six people.

Derek: Did he?

Rita: Didn't you ever hear about it?

Derek: No!

Rita: Oh yes, he shot six people. He was in a big rage. He got a pony and trap and – clever watchmaker my grandfather was – and he found out that my grandmother…[489] The publican of the pub in Castle Street,[490] he bought my grandmother a shop,[491] and my

479 Amy Moss (1888-1972), sister of Rose and Rita's aunt.
480 Elsie Moss (1891-1969), sister of Rose and Rita's aunt.
481 Herbert James Style, son of Oliver and Harriett, and Rita's father.
482 Norman Style (1904-1984), Rita's brother and Derek's father.
483 Edith Harriett Style (1868-1953), daughter of Oliver and Harriett.
484 Elizabeth Jane Style (1870-1954), daughter of Oliver and Harriett.
485 Oliver Thomas Style (1867-1905), son of Oliver and Harriett.
486 These are the children of Oliver and Harriett who lived after 1899, when Rita was born.
487 This is not correct; Oliver Thomas Style was the eldest, but Rita would not have known him as he died when she was five years old.
488 Oliver Style.
489 Harriett, Oliver's wife.
490 The Elephant and Castle, 23 Castle Street, Hillfields.
491 The Castle Stores, next door at No. 25. Harriett is listed here in the 1901

grandfather didn't like the fact that he bought her that shop and then he found out she was having 'to do' with the publican.[492] So, my grandfather had got some rooms. You remember the Scala in Coventry?[493] You remember that court with rooms at the top? My grandfather's watchmaking place was at the top. Well, he went out and bought a gun, and was in his pony and trap and he shot at six people, and my auntie Doris,[494] she'd got a friend Chataway, and her father had to have his leg off.[495] Well, my grandfather went to prison, and when he came out of prison he did so want to see my Dad,[496] and my grandmother wouldn't allow my grandfather to see [him].

Derek: So what happened then?

Rita: Oh, he ran off with the nurse from prison. Went off to London and married her. So, whether she's alive and he's alive and they live in London, I don't know.[497]

Derek: It's a long time ago.[498]

Rita: That happened to my grandfather. He had to go to prison. Didn't you know that?

Derek: No.

and 1911 census returns, while the landlord of the Elephant and Castle was Thomas Bates.

492 This seems unlikely, as the reason for Oliver and Harriett separating was his jealousy over her talking with Henry White and Walter Goddard in the Old Half Moon in 1879, and Harriett wasn't in the Castle Stores until some time between the 1891 and 1901 census returns, when Oliver had already been in prison for a decade or more.

493 Opened in 1913, the Scala was renamed the Odeon in 1950. It was converted to a Rank Bingo club and demolished in 1973 following fire damage.

494 Doris Emily Moss (1900-1974), sister of Rita's mother Rose.

495 Henry Jennings. His daughters married men named Clarke, Wilson and Gough, so it's unclear who the 'Chataway' is that Rita had in mind; she may simply have misremembered the name.

496 Rita means her brother Herbert Charles Style, who had just been born.

497 As we've seen, Oliver was admitted to the Coventry Union Workhouse soon after his visit to see his grandson, and left only when transferred to Hatton Asylum.

498 A kindly understatement – Oliver would have been one-hundred-and-thirty-eight years old had he been alive at the time of this interview!

Rita: Oh, Doris[499] ought to have told you. Oh yes, and one man had to have his leg off.

Derek: So where were they living when all that happened?

Rita: They were living in Stoke Park.[500] They had a smashing place. He had his watchmaking place in Loughborough High, opposite the Scala.

Derek: it sounds as though he'd got a bit of money then. Had he?

Rita: Oh yes, he'd got a bit of money. And she still carried on with the publican. She was a lass my grandma was.

Derek: That would be in the papers wouldn't it?

Rita: It was in the papers. It was in all the Coventry papers. If you could get a paper from that time... How long did he go in for? The fact that one had his leg off. When he came out he did so want to see my Dad.[501] My [brother] was the one he wanted to see. And he went to see my mother and my mother let him hold my [brother]. Of course, he was only young then.

Derek: Who was it he wanted to see?

Rita: Rogue,[502] and mother let him hold him and my Dad[503] walked in and he didn't half get it. Anyway, about two months after he went off to London with the nurse from the prison, went to live there. And my grandmother still carried on with the shop and she'd still got her fancy man at the pub next door.

Derek: Do you know what his name was?

Rita: Charles, wasn't it? Charles Styles.[504]

Derek: Because grandad was Herbert Charles, wasn't he?

Rita: Ooh, he was handsome, my grandfather.

Rita: And then when my grandma[505] died she left me two

499 Derek's mother Doris May Green (1908-1991), wife of Norman Style and therefore sister-in-law to Rita.

500 Actually Harnall Row, off Far Gosford Street.

501 *Sic*: Rita means his grandson Herbert Charles Style, born six months after Oliver was released from prison.

502 The nickname of Herbert Charles Style.

503 Herbert James Style, Oliver's son.

504 *Sic*: Oliver Style.

505 Harriett.

cottages. She had this housekeeper, and you know Nelson Street in Coventry? She'd got a brother[506] who'd got a lot of old cottages down Nelson Street. They'd got money all of them. My grandmother had a woman looking after her, so when my grandmother died[507] she left me two cottages, and my Dad came back from the funeral and he said, "Rita, you don't want those cottages." He said, "Let your Gran's housekeeper have them." So, I said, "Oh I don't want them," You know, being young and bloody silly. "I don't want them Dad. It's alright, she can have them." Do you know, she still lived in the two cottages? They were sort of joined together, only a sort of kitchen and sitting room. Kitchen on the other. The baker on the corner, he wanted to buy them after, and do you know she got an enormous amount of money for those two cottages – and I'd let her have them.

Derek: It should have gone to you should it?

Rita: Oh, I didn't bother, I just let her have them, and then of course she sold them after, for I think two or three thousand. I've done some silly things. I've let quite a bit of money go.

Derek: What was your grandma's name?

Rita: Harriett.

Derek: That was the one that was married to Charles?

Rita: Yes, my grandfather's name was Charles Styles[508] and he shot six people and one man had to have his leg off and it was our Doris's uncle that had to have his leg off. Our Doris[509] – Mrs Burr – her friend's uncle had to have his leg off. We've had some tragedy. I'll tell you this much. My dad should have... He sat up night after night after night inventing the silk. You know, it was all pure silk then, and Dad found out a way for the imitation silk and instead of Dad taking it out, he left it for a bit and Cluleys got it. You know

506 Probably Walter Elkington (1850-1941). Harriett's other brothers were James, who had died in 1892, and Thomas, who had moved to Wales by 1891 and died there in 1901. Walter lived at Upper Nelson Street in 1891, and at 57 Castle Street in 1901, when Harriett was at No. 25.

507 In 1929.

508 *Sic*: Oliver Style.

509 Doris Emily Moss.

what Cluleys did with Dad? They gave him so much money more a week on his pension. He should have had the big amount. My Dad was clever. Your grandfather was clever.

Derek: What was his trade? Did he have a trade?

Rita: Oh, I don't know.

Derek: It sounds as though he was an engineer.

Rita: He used to sit night after night, but of course he had asthma.

Derek: I remember that.

Rita: And that was the trouble. He sat night after night on this invention and then didn't have it at the finish. He let where he worked have it – Clarke Cluleys.[510] So, then we came to live at the farm. Dad had got the pension and Dad had got asthma very bad. The first doctor we had – we lived at Limes Farm – the first doctor we had – Doctor Gateley – he came to see Dad, and he said to Dad – "You'd be troubled without it." My Dad said, "I wish you'd got it." So old Gateley went off, and he said to his partner, the other doctor, he said, "I've had a bit this morning. Old Styles told me I'd be sorry if I'd got asthma." That doctor's still alive, I often see him. He suffers with his stomach. We were at the Limes Farm for quite a bit.

Derek: You came out because of the Blitz didn't you?

Rita: Yes, we went to Leicester to stay with Hubert and Mabel.[511]

Derek: They were there first, were they?

Rita: And Doris went to… where did Doris and Norman go?[512]

Derek: To Kenilworth, and then to Leamington.

Rita: But didn't they first of all go to Corley Moor to live with somebody?

Derek: They went to a place called Brandon. Everybody was getting out of Coventry at that time, weren't they?

Rita: Of course, they were.

Derek: Where were you living before you left Coventry?

510 Clarke, Cluley & Co. were a prominent car manufacturer based in Coventry. They were founded in 1890 as an engineering firm. Herbert Style was employed making pumps.

511 Mabel Agnes Moss (1893-1966), sister of Rose and aunt to Rita.

512 Norman and Doris Style, Derek's parents.

Rita: We'd got our own house.

Derek: Where was that?

Rita: In Saxon Road over at Walsgrave. We'd got a lovely house. We had a friend that built me a miniature golf course. I started to play golf. We had every fruit tree imaginable because we'd got such a big garden, and he made us a miniature golf course and I used to have all the Rugbyites on a Sunday afternoon. But I got tired of that, making cups of tea for all of them, and then from there we went to stay at Mabel's for a bit in Leicester, and then mother got the big house at the back of the Co-op and I went to live with mother.

Derek: Fox Hollies.

Rita: I got a cottage, but when I got this cottage it was empty and I had it done up and...

Derek: You had a lot of furniture in there, didn't you?

Rita: Oh yes, I had a lot of furniture in there, but a friend... of course they couldn't get me out of the cottage, as I was always at my mother's, and Mrs Greville said, "Certainly not, she's a good tenant." Anyway, I did get the cottage at the side of the farm and everybody used to look in the window. I used to have a lot of [inaudible]. I had some fun. I used to go dancing.

Derek: You say you were in Saxon Road in Walsgrave? How long were you there?

Rita: We had just put the deposit on another house. We were going at the back of the station. Of course, Bertie[513] moved to Birmingham and we were going at the back of the station. Well we didn't have that house, it was a bigger house altogether. Well, then when Bertie was at Birmingham he sent word to say that he'd got a house for us. We had to pay so much a year and it was a lovely big house, but it was at the back of the town, in a cul-de-sac. All fields at the back of the town. It was a dear house Bertie had bought us – £2,000 at that time.

Derek: Was that for Gran as well? Was it just for you and him, or

513 Rita's husband, Charles Bertie Houghton Clare (1894-1965).

was it for the family as well?

Rita: No, it was for Bertie and I. Bertie brought the car. Bertie took the car to show us this house. It was a nice house. It had a laundry and everything, but I said, "I don't want a laundry, no thank you," and I refused it. And he said, "Now look here, it's a nice house and you've refused it," and I said, "And it's at the back of the town, the war's on, and I'm going to the farm to my mother and dad" and I did, but he said, "I shall never get you another house," and he didn't. But he came here. Bertie lived here for quite a time when he was ill.

Derek: Did he work in Coventry?

Rita: Bertie worked at the GEC. When he went to Birmingham, Bertie was head of them all at Birmingham. He was over all the men. I'll show you his photograph. He was over any amount of men, and do you know, Bertie's club at Birmingham at Erdington, about twelve months ago it was burnt to the ground, all the wines and spirits and Bertie was over it all. He lived here for quite a time before he died.

Derek: Do you know something, I've never heard of this uncle Oliver.[514]

Rita: Your uncle Oliver? He was a handsome man. He went to Birmingham. They reckon he was the most handsome man in Coventry. My Dad was nice-looking when he was younger. We had a lovely photograph of my father. I don't know what became of it. We enjoyed living at the back of the Co-op in Sharnford. But we moved about a bit. Where I was going to live was a nice part of Birmingham at the back of the town. When you come to weigh it up, it's all under the bridge now.

Derek: That's why I'd like to find out about it before it gets too late to find out.

Rita: Bertie came and he took Dad, mother, and we'd got a place over Gee Hill. It was a big house with a laundry. For a start I said I didn't want a big laundry because I didn't – I'd got no children.

514 Possibly referring to Rita's uncle Oliver Thomas Style.

Derek: Mind you, did you say Lizzie and Edie went back to Birmingham?

Rita: Aunt Lizzie has still got some relatives alive there. I bet Aunt Lizzie's daughter, Edith, she lives in Bordesley Green.

Derek: What was her married name?

Rita: And her brother,[515] was head of the Birmingham Post Office.

Derek: What was Lizzie's name when she got married? Do you remember?

Rita: I couldn't tell you. And then there was Alfie,[516] he looked after the art gallery. That was Aunt Lizzie's son, Alf, and he was a bit of a rascal. But he got the job looking after the attendants at the art gallery in Birmingham. He was a proper lad he was, and the old King George went round one day and my uncle Alf said to him "Crikey I don't know how you've got your job. You've a queer old soul aren't you?" But he was up the art gallery for quite a time. Aunt Lizzie's son got to be head of the main post office.

Derek: Lizzie's husband was called Alf, was he?

Rita: What happened to him? I think he died. What was his surname?

Derek: Whereabouts in Birmingham did they live – do you remember?

Rita: There's somebody lives at Bordesley Green now. They've altered it. It's quite a nice place now. One of Dad's relatives who's still alive lives at Earlsbury Gardens, Perry Barr. One or two of Edith's relatives live there, opposite the big police station. And do you know I had a cousin – I used to go over sometime to my aunt Edith's in Perry Barr and the police station was opposite and one day somebody came to aunt Edith and said, "Have you seen your daughter?" and aunt Edith said, "No, I haven't seen her lately, where is she Rita?" and I said, "Well she went out," because I was staying there at the time. She'd only climbed up the police station – my cousin. She was a card. And you know my uncle[517] had got a fancy

515 Aunt Lizzie's son, Alpha James Lewis (1891-1960).
516 Alpha James Lewis.
517 Probably James Lapworth, husband of Edith Harriet Style.

woman. They lived in a big house, and my uncle had got a factory. A plating factory. They used to do the handlebars on the bikes. Well he'd got this factory and he'd got a fancy woman, and suddenly instead of a lovely fur coat going to wherever it was supposed to go, it was going to this fancy woman. My aunt Edith found out, and do you know what she did? She went and bought the poshest fur coat she could find in the shops at Birmingham and bought it and sent the bill to my uncle – so my uncle not only had one fur coat to pay for, he had the two.

Derek: Serves him right.

Rita: I've had some relatives! I'll tell you. But I enjoyed Sharnford. I started to go down to the New Inn with Dolly, but then of course I hurt my back. They are always asking about me. They'd be glad to see me. Anyway. I've had joy. I'll be glad when I can get straighter. I'm getting straighter.

Derek: Have you seen the doctor about it?

Rita: No, he's never bothered with me.

Derek: Well you've got to tell him, you know.

Rita: All he did was give me some tablets, because I lay on the floor for three days and I've never seen him since. I've never bothered. If I can get my back straight.

Derek: You ought to tell him.

Rita: Ah, he's a black doctor. We've got two black doctors here as well as the white. So, there you go. You have that don't you? Anyway, it's nice to see you. You'll come again won't you?

Derek: Of course, we will. As I say, we shall be in the area quite a lot really because we're looking at the records and the churches for Pat's relatives. Probably I shall have a look for mine while I'm about it. Because Mum says that Charles, your granddad, is buried in Coventry cemetery.[518]

Rita: He is, yes.

Derek: So he should be in the records there.

Rita: Yes, he would be in the records there. They are all in there,

518 *Sic*: Oliver Style was buried in the cemetery at Hatton Asylum.

aren't they? I tell you who went in there… I had a baby and the baby was put in the same grave as my grandma.[519] I remember that. Because they always put the babies in there. I lost it. I only had the one child.

Derek: Was it very old?

Rita: It died at birth, and Bertie had to carry it up to the cemetery.

Derek: How sad.

Rita: He didn't go in the car. He didn't want to. He was very sad about us losing the baby. I never had any more. I was told that I shouldn't have any more. I had a terrific birth. Worse things happen though, don't they?

Derek: It's not so bad nowadays. I think women these days have an easier time.

Rita: They do. Do you know what was the cause of me losing the baby? I had an old doctor, and I'd been to see the doctor the night before and I was going into Marlborough Nursing Home at the time to have the baby, and that was just across the road at Marlborough Road. Well, my water had broken and he didn't have the sense to tell me. So, when I got home I walked from Saxon Road to the hospital, and my water had broken and I lost the baby. Other than that, I was going to wait till it was time and go into Marlborough Nursing Home. I remember all those things. But there you go, you lose them and that's that. So, I was told I shouldn't have any more children, and then when Bertie bought me this big house in Birmingham I though fancy me having a blasted laundry.

Derek: You wouldn't need it. They had big families.

Rita: You know what he'd got a mind to? He wanted to be an artist, because he was a lovely painter. Mrs Kibble's still got a pair of paintings that Bertie had done, and she really prized them. Bertie was an artist. He could paint like [inaudible]. Fancy me having a big house with a laundry. You had to pay so much every year to the Council, but you'd got to buy it. So, he said he would never buy me another house. So I said OK, then mother moved into the farm and I moved into the cottage. Do you know that there's one thing

519 Harriett is buried at Coventry's London Road Cemetery.

in my life that I can always feel sad about? We had a little dog, do you remember? Bob.

Derek: Yes, a Collie.

Rita: We bought him from Coventry to the farm, and there was a dog that was lame at the farm, and the first thing he did, he went biting our Bob. I used to go every day to take Bob out. At the finish, Bob wasn't very well and I thought, "I don't know how I'm going to tell our mother but Bob's being sick," and I used to take him out every day. I thought I'll have him put to sleep, because he can't go on like this, and I can see that day now and I always regretted it. I thought, "Rita you've got to do it." And I said to Mr Horton, "Will you put our dog down? I don't like doing it and I don't know how to tell my mother, but he's very poorly." And as I was speaking to Arthur Horton, the farmer here, Bob was sick and he could see he was poorly. So, when I got home I said, "I'm sorry but I've had the dog put down," and do you know, it was like as though my mother never forgave me. And I always regretted after and I let him. Arthur put him to sleep. If he had died in the night, but my Dad and mother only had the apartment. And I've always seen our poor Bob, walking off with this Arthur Horton, and that's one thing I never like to think about in my life. Mind you he was old, he was about 13 or 14.

Derek: That's a good age for a dog.

Rita: Do you have a dog?

Pat: We had one. We had to have him put down about three months ago. He started being sick all over the place. They said it was his kidneys going wrong, and we had to take him to the vet and have him put down.

Rita: Oh that's a relief. Because Arthur Horton was a vet.

Pat: You can't do anything else.

Derek: He was sick all the time and the vet gave him some tablets, and when he took the tablets he wasn't sick, but he was making a mess everywhere. And if you stopped the tablets, he started being sick again. It was always something. And the other thing was, when we went on holiday Mum and Dad – Doris and Norman – used to look after the dog, and of course you can't ask them to look after a dog that's being sick all the time. So, we had him put down.

Rita: So, it's exactly the same thing. My mother did create but I couldn't do anything.

Pat: I think it happens to a lot of them about that age. Thirteen for a dog is quite old.

Rita: What's the time?

Derek: Two minutes before four o'clock.

Rita: Have you got your car?

Derek: I suppose we'll have to be going in a bit.

Rita: You've not got some odd change?

Derek: We've got piles of odd change.

[Interference from another recording on the tape]

Derek: You shouldn't bother really.

Rita: Well let's have it. It's only money.

Derek: All right then. Thank you very much.

Rita: I usually have odd bits all over the place. Odd bits of money.

Pat: Do you have any photographs of your father?

Rita: When Aunt Amy died, mother had got lots of photographs of the family and everything but I don't know what became of them. Of course, that woman would had them. Do you know what happened? In Ethel's[520] will there was me, there was Stan, there was about four of us in Ethel's will. Ray, our cousin Ray.[521] Anyway, suddenly it came out as she had turned the will over to the woman who was looking after her. So, somebody turned round to me and said, "It's no good you looking for anything from Ethel's will, she's turned it over to Mrs Lewy." I said "What! She's only just been getting her a bit of dinner." But she'd wheedled round our Ethel. So, I met her going up for her pension so I said, "Look here, you flipping old twister. You'll never be able to put your head comfortably on the pillow." Because there was Ray, there was four of us in Ethel's will. Anyway, the next day her daughter came up to me – her stepdaughter mind you – and she said, "Fancy you telling

520 Ethel Moss (1895-1981), sister of Rita's mother Rose, and therefore her aunt.

521 Raymond Hubert Collins (1927-2007), son of Rita's Aunt Mabel.

my mother that she won't be able to put her head on the pillow." So I said, "Nor will you." She said, "There's only mother and I having Ethel's money," and none of us went to Ethel's funeral, none of us. Ray never went to Ethel's funeral – none of us.

Derek: And you think all the photographs…

Rita: And now she lives down here in one of these houses, and do you know what she had done? A Wendy house built along the garden. This daughter, the way she came up and said, "It's no good you telling my mother she won't put her head on the pillow – you won't benefit." They had all Ethel's money, and the woman in the nursing home – Ethel had to go into the nursing home at the finish – and Mrs Williams at the nursing home came to see me, and she said, "I can't understand you, Mrs Clare. Why didn't you set to and do something about Ethel's will, because every time they went in to see her, she was saying to them, "When are you going to bring my money in?" So that's what happened with Ethel's money, and Ethel left a nice old penny. Our Ray said, "You want to contest it." Ray Collins – fancy, his Dad is ninety-four[522] – he wanted to contest it. I didn't want to, I don't believe in it. I thought if it's been done like that, but I did tell her that she'd never put her head on the pillow. And ever since she's been ill.

Derek: You've put a curse on her did you?

Rita: I think she thought I had, when the daughter came up.

Derek: So, you think all the photographs went with her.

Rita: I don't know what happened to the photographs. My mother was a beautiful woman. She went as Primrose and Ivy. [Kevitt] Rotherham, the lawyer, fell head over heels in love with mother. Rotherham would have liked to marry my mother, but my mother was crazy for my Dad. Look at Rotherham now, it's a big firm.

Derek: She lived in Hillfields as a young girl, didn't she?

Rita: My grandma lived in Hillfields. She had a greengrocery shop, and the pub next door was her fancy man. He bought it her

522 Ray's father, Hubert Edward Collins, was born in October 1891, but as this conversation took place in the early 1980s Rita was incorrect about his age.

and my granddad went to prison. He shot at six people, and one man had to have his leg off. It was funny that the man who was named Curtis and was aunty Doris's friend. That's how things go. When we came here, Bertie was coming over from Birmingham and he suddenly regretted this house by his club. He was head of his club when he died, in Birmingham, and they had a bowling green, swimming pool and when he died it was burnt to the ground, so I don't know how they're going on. But all that drink over there. They used to bring me a cupboard full of drink every year. Would you like a drink?

Derek: No, thank you, I'm driving. You're not allowed to drink and drive now you know. You get put in prison if you drink anything.

Rita: Bertie was secretary of this club. A lovely club it is. It's still there, being rebuilt. There is a relative, there's my cousin and his brother still alive in Birmingham, somewhere in Bordesley Green.

Derek: It's a pity you can't remember the name after she got marred.

Rita: I can't remember. What was our Lizzie's name? I think it might be Lewis, and the eldest son was an attendant at the art gallery. He saw the old King George go round the art gallery and he said, "You've never seen such a crazy old devil." He said he was really soppy. He was a proper lad my cousin Alf. He used to walk from Birmingham to Coventry every week with a couple of pound of sausage for my dad. My dad liked the Birmingham pork sausage, so he used to walk every week, instead of riding on the bus. We're a funny lot. We've let money go. She never looks at me now. She lives down here now. She's gone in the house next door to Ethel and she's had a Wendy house built, and she goes away with the money. Hubert reckoned Ethel left about £50,000 between us. There was Hubert, myself, Ray.

Derek: It's a shame. It leaves a lot of bad feeling.

Rita: I've got money of my own, so I don't care.

Derek: As long as you've got enough, that's all that matters.

Rita: I've got enough. In fact, I've got more than enough. I still think of what I could do with it. I was going to send that to Norman to sit in the conservatory, because Doris has had a new place put on now, but then when he was taken ill it wasn't so… Fancy, Hubert at ninety-four. He still lives in Birmingham, and he's got the pub next door so he can just walk out of one place to another. Of course, he's all whisky.

Derek: Where's that?

Rita: Leicester and Ray is still at the mining. He's not a miner, he's an overseer. Where does Ray live? He was over here the other week. He didn't come here, but he went to a relative outside Coventry.

Derek: Shall I tell you something that Norma told me? Norma said that your Dad wasn't born in Coventry, he came from Birmingham.

Rita: No. Perhaps he did, but he did live in Coventry. My grandfather did live in Coventry in Stoke Park. He may not have been born in Coventry. My grandfather was a clever man, very clever. When he got into trouble my grandmother went on beading for Courtaulds. She was a lovely beader, she used to do the beading in the dresses and all that sort of thing. But my grandma Style was very austere. Anyway, she left me two cottages. That's how I started, on two cottages put in Lloyds Bank. I had a baby and Bertie carried it up to the cemetery and had it put it with… I don't regret not having children. They're nice to have, but you get as you live without them.

Derek: The Styles have never been great ones for having lots of children. My mother, Doris, she has six brothers and sisters, and then her mum and dad had lots and lots of relatives, but the Styles didn't seem to bother. You were one of three, and that's unusual because most people were having six and seven and eight in those days. And then you had one, and my mother had two and Norma didn't have any, and Rogue didn't have any. I haven't got any relatives, have I?

Rita: No, there wasn't a lot from us was there?

Derek: It's surprising that, isn't it? I'm rather surprised my gran didn't have more children.

Rita: The thing I really regretted was I let those cottages go, and then there was that woman and she sold them to the baker on Nelson Street for a lot of money. Of course, she made Lloyds' bakery down Nelson Street. My grandmother had some money left her. Her brother was a chappy named Elkington that had got other property, and my grandmother had had some left her so that went to the baker. Do you know, that baker used to deal bread to us and he used to come round with the bread, it was lovely bread, and he'd stand and listened to my mother singing. Do you know Rotherham, where you're going. I don't mind if you mention it. Kevitt Rotherham[523] met my mother at a ball. She went as Primrose, my grandmother had dressed her in... the photograph is somewhere, I'll see if I can get it... and she went to the ball and Kevitt Rotherham was there and he wanted to have my mother trained in Turner's opera company. My mother had got the most beautiful signing voice anybody could listen to, and the baker used to come round and forget all his bakery and stand in the yard and listen to my mother signing. She got married to my dad and she was a wasted woman. Rotherham would have had her trained at Turner's opera company.

Derek: Why did she go for granddad then instead of Rotherham?

Rita: Well my Dad was very nice-looking as a young man

Derek: She was spoiled for choice, was she? She wasn't very old when she got wed, was she?

Rita: She was only sixteen when she married my Dad.

Derek: How old was he?

Rita: He was about twenty-one. But Kevitt Rotherham, the lawyer, he loved my mother, He'd have had her trained. And the baker and everyone used to listen to my mother, and then once they joined a choir, my dad and mother. They went to Earlsdon Club[524] in Coventry and my mother and dad were singing there. My dad had got a nice tenor voice, but my mother sang 'Bartin' on her own. And when my mother had finished at this club – the Earlsdon Club, it's still there – they threw their hats up. They went crazy for my mother singing. She was absolutely beautiful that night. The next

523 Kevitt Rotherham (1864-1950) was a member of the famous Coventry watch and clockmaking family Rotherham and Sons.

524 Originally the Earlsdon Coffee Tavern on Earlsdon Street, it was renamed the Earlsdon Working Men's Club and later the Albany Social Club.

The Earlsdon Coffee Tavern,
where Rita's mother received a rapturous reception.

day my uncle Tom, the watchmaker from Spon Street who'd got the watch firm, he came and begged her to go with him to see the manager of the club, but she wouldn't go. My mother had the most glorious voice anyone could listen to. She was contralto, she could have gone in opera. She sang 'Bartin'. My uncle Tom Taylor[525] came several times, and he said they all threw their hats up. Some days she used to be in the kitchen and she'd be singing. She never liked housework or anything like that. I don't like housework. They came several times after my mother. Dad had got a nice tenor signing

525 Thomas Alfred Taylor (b1850).

voice. They were both good singers.

Derek: You had an Uncle Tom as well did you?

Rita: Uncle Tom had a big watchmaking place down in Coventry. You know the Spon End bridges in Coventry? You walk up past the yard to the Chain[526] and my uncle Tom had a detached house and used to make watches and clocks. My grandfather was a watchmaker.

Derek: Was that on your mother's side?

Rita: On my mother's side.

Derek: I thought there were only sisters, you know.

Rita: But he was uncle to them all – uncle Tom Taylor. He had two watchmaking places, one by the Chain and one up higher. He put a man named Adams in that one to manage it, but they all came to sticky ends, squandered or something.

Derek: Can you remember your mother's mother and father?

Rita: Grandma Moss and my grandfather. He used to sit up in the back bedroom making watches. He was a watchmaker. My mother had plenty of sisters, Amy, Elsie, Ethel. Mother was the eldest.

Derek: If you look at those, there's not that many children. Amy never married.

Elsie married but Amy didn't.

Rita: Elsie's dead. They are all dead. Ted has died now. I could never understand that will of Ethel's. Our Ethel left a nice little penny. You'd have wanted to contest it. But it's too late now. She sold two houses together and she's had it. Not that any of us bother after. We let it go, but we could have contested it. It would have cost us a bit to contest it, but there you go, we didn't. I'm crossing my fingers. I've never wanted for money.

Derek: As long as you've got enough to get by on you don't need

526 The Coventry Chain Company was incorporated in the late 1890s as a bicycle chain producer. Registered as a private limited company in 1902, the business purchased premises at Spon End, alongside the arches, in 1907 and began producing chains for all engineering purposes. By the Great War it had begun manufacturing track chains for use on tank. The company eventually merged with Hans Renold Ltd, and in 1931 was listed as the Renold and Coventry Chain Company Limited.

too much, do you?

Rita: No, you don't have to have too much. If they find out that you've got too much money they start putting your rent up. You don't have to say. I don't say how much money I have, because they start putting your rent up. And yet the lady next door to me doesn't pay rent.

Derek: It depends how much you've got put by. That's the problem with my father, Norman. He's alright at the moment because he's got nothing put by, but if he had a lot of money he'd be paying to be in his house.

Rita: Your Dad's alright for money, isn't he?

Derek: He doesn't need a lot.

Rita: Doris won't want.

Derek: No, she's alright.

Rita: As long as she's alright. I'd soon send money. I think I gave her fifty pounds. I wouldn't let her go without money, if I knew she wanted it. She must have a bit by. Has she got some money? If she hasn't I'll send her some.

Derek: She's alright, she'll get by. She hasn't got a lot.

Rita: She has a bit of supplementary.

Derek: She has a pension of nineteen pounds a week, and a supplementary of nineteen pounds a week.

Rita: That isn't a lot for that house.

Derek: It's enough.

Pat: The trouble is the social service limit. If she's got any extra they won't give her supplementary benefit. It's very tricky isn't it? So, we have to keep an eye on it.

Derek: You see Mum's got a few hundred put by, but it's in my name, in my bank really so that the social services don't know it's there, because if they know she's got it then she won't get her supplementary benefit.

Rita: I see. Well I don't get supplementary. I don't get a scrap of anything.

Derek: But Mum does, but I've got this tucked away and Norma's got a bit tucked away for her as well. If you wanted Dad to have some in your will you ought to make me a trustee or something, then it can be tucked away for him.

Rita: I'll see into that. I'll ask Hubert about that when he comes over.

Derek: I'll go and see Rotherham's if you want.

Rita: Ask Rotherham how Doris goes on, because Doris comes into Norman's. Anytime now I can go to Rotherham's in the car with Dolly and her husband, but I don't want to, until I feel right.

Derek: Anyway, we can always get Rotherham's to come and see you, if you wanted.

Rita: Oh no, I don't want to. He's got my will. I'll just have things changed.

Derek: You've got to see him or he's got to see you. You can't just get them changed without going to see him. I can go and talk to him, but I can't change your will for you.

Rita: I don't want the will changed. Only if anything happens to Norman. If Norman got better then Norman is alright, but if he doesn't get better then Norman's money… I've got a bit of ready cash round here. I don't go without money round me. I've got a nice lot of new notes but I keep those. I don't let anybody have those. But there you go, such is life. You don't know what is coming to you.

Derek: As far as my father's concerned, he's more concerned about the big picture than he is about money. You know that big picture that you've got?

Rita: That picture's mine! I wouldn't have been able to have it. And it isn't a painting, it's a lithograph.[527]

Derek: It's the sentimental value you see.

Rita: Doris is fuelling him over that. But it's mine. And until it goes that is mine, but the others are real oil paintings. My oil paintings are worth a thousand pounds more than that lithograph. It's the sentimental value, but mother gave it to me, so what's given to me is mine! But Granny Moses as a youngster started to paint, and she's one of the biggest painters in America now. Well that's that Indian girl that side. This one is by somebody Vergony. He's a

527 This picture, entitled 'Hush', was believed within the family to have been valuable. Rita is standing alongside it in the photograph on page 133.

good Italian painter. That's worth plenty of money, my paintings are worth plenty of money, but what the lithograph would be worth I do not know, but it's my picture. If I wanted to leave that picture to you I could. Doris couldn't touch it. Doris wanted it.

Derek: What are you going to do with it then?

Rita: I don't know what I'm going to do. My will's made with Rotherham. I've made my will out and you benefit by my will, Norma benefits by my will, Doris benefits by my will, but that lithograph is mine!

BIBLIOGRAPHY

PRIMARY SOURCES

The National Archives

ASSI 11/33: Assizes: Midland Circuit: Crown Minute Books: 1873 Winter-1882 Winter

ASSI 12/13: Assizes: Midland Circuit: Indictment Files

Warwickshire Archives

Warwickshire County Record Office: CR 1664/351/1-2

Warwickshire County Record Office: CR 1664/516 (Notices of Deaths of Patients)

Warwickshire County Record Office: CR 1664/551 (Register of Burials at the Asylum)

Other Primary Sources

1939 Register; Baptism records; Birth records; Census returns 1841-1911; Marriage records; Death records

Army Registers of Soldiers' Effects, 1901-1929

Calendar of Prisoners, 1868-1929

Camden Workhouse Register, 1818-1843

Criminal Registers, 1791-1892: Warwickshire, 1843/1844

Life expectancy at Birth, England and Wales, 1841 to 2011: Office of National Statistics.

National Archives Currency Convertor

National Probate Calendar

Newgate Calendar of Prisoners

Lunacy Patients Admission Registers, 1846-1912
Prison Commission Records, 1770-1951. Pentonville Prison: Register of Prisoners
Registers of Habitual Criminals and Police Gazettes, 1834-1934
WWI Pension Ledgers and Index Cards, 1914-1923
WWI Service Medal and Award Rolls, 1914-1923

SECONDARY SOURCES

Newspapers, Journals and Directories

Ashby-de-la-Zouch Gazette
Atherstone, Nuneaton and Warwickshire Times
Birmingham Daily Post
British Medical Journal
Cheltenham Mercury
Coleshill Chronicle
Coventry Evening Telegraph
Coventry Herald
Coventry Herald and Free Press
Coventry Herald and Observer
Coventry Standard
Coventry Times
Glasgow Evening Post
Kelly's Directory of Warwickshire
Kenilworth Advertiser
Leamington Spa Courier
Liverpool Mercury
Medical Directory
Midland Daily Telegraph
Midwife's Register
Portsmouth Evening News
South Wales Daily News
Trade Directories
Warwickshire Herald

Books

Ashby, John (2001): *The Character of Coventry*

Carter, Terry (2012): *Birmingham Pals: 14th, 15th & 16th (Service) Battalions of the Royal Warwickshire Regiment, A History of the Three City Battalions Raised in Birmingham in World War One*

Fry, David and Smith, Albert (2011): *The Coventry We Have Lost: Earlsdon and Chapelfields Explored*

Legg, D.R.G. (2000): *Portland Prison Illustrated (1848-2000)*

McGrory, David (2013): *Bloody British History: Coventry*

Moments in Time: The History of the Coventry Watch Industry Volume 1 by the Coventry Watch Museum Project Limited (5th Edition: 2014)

Montes, Mary: *Brown Boots in Earlsdon* (Coventry and Warwickshire Historical Association Pamphlet No. 15)

Owens, Lewis (2018): *The Pentonville Experiment: Prison. Addiction. Hope.*

The Coventry Watchmakers' Heritage Trail: A Guided Walk Through the Watchmaking Areas of Spon End and Chapelfields in Coventry by the Coventry Watch …eum Project Limited (3rd Revised Edition: 2014)

West, Ian: 'Isle of Portland Quarries - Geology'. University of Southampton

Websites

www.capitalpunishment.uk.org

www.countyasylums.co.uk/central-hospital-hatton

www.coventrysociety.org.uk

www.earlsdon.org.uk

www.historiccoventry.co.uk

www.institutionalhistory.com

INDEX